EFFECTIVE LIFECYCLE MANAGEMENT OF HEALTHCARE APPLICATIONS

Utilizing a Portfolio Framework

EFFECTIVE LIFECYCLE MANAGEMENT OF HEALTHCARE APPLICATIONS

Utilizing a Portfolio Framework

Susan M. Houston, MBA, RN-BC, PMP, CPHIMS, FHIMSS

Ryan D. Kennedy, BS

CRC Press
Taylor & Francis Group
Boca Raton London New York

CRC Press is an imprint of the
Taylor & Francis Group, an **informa** business

A PRODUCTIVITY PRESS BOOK

Cover Art by Nix Houston

CRC Press
Taylor & Francis Group
6000 Broken Sound Parkway NW, Suite 300
Boca Raton, FL 33487-2742

© 2020 by Taylor & Francis Group, LLC
CRC Press is an imprint of Taylor & Francis Group, an Informa business

No claim to original U.S. Government works
Printed on acid-free paper

International Standard Book Number-13: 978-0-367-37445-7 (Hardback)
International Standard Book Number-13: 978-0-367-37389-4 (Paperback)

Visit the Taylor & Francis Web site at
http://www.taylorandfrancis.com

and the CRC Press Web site at
http://www.crcpress.com

Contents

Acknowledgments

I would like to thank my family for their ongoing support and understanding. For my husband, you are my rock and you are always there with words of wisdom or sarcasm, whichever is appropriate. For my children, Nicole, Nick, Matt, and Dana, thank you for always being there whenever I needed encouragement. To Ryan, you are a good friend and always a pleasure to work with.

—Susan M. Houston

First and foremost, I need to thank my amazing wife, Megan. Your support has been unwavering, from reviewing draft chapters to removing all distractions for hours (and even days) at a time. I never could have done this without you. To my children, Alex and Katie, you are everything to me – and now we have an exciting new bedtime story to read! To my mentor and friend, Sue, you have guided my career. Thank you for giving me every possible opportunity to succeed.

—Ryan D. Kennedy

We would both like to thank Nix Houston for the wonderful cover art.

Authors

Susan M. Houston is a senior consultant in healthcare IT after retiring as the Chief of the Portfolio Office within the Department of Clinical Research Informatics at the National Institutes of Health Clinical Center. Her background includes clinical nursing, informatics, and project and portfolio management. Houston has presented workshops and lectures at several local, regional, national, and international conferences and meetings. She has authored a variety of articles and books on project management and informatics. She is a member of the Project Management Institute (PMI), American Nursing Informatics Association (ANIA), and the Healthcare Information and Management Systems Society (HIMSS), while serving on various committees.

Ryan D. Kennedy is the Acting Chief of the Project and Portfolio Office at the National Institutes of Health Clinical Center and an instructor for an IT Project Management course at the University of Maryland, School of Nursing. Kennedy's project work has contributed to the implementation of new clinical systems, infrastructure upgrades, and improved workflow processes. In addition, he has presented workshops and lectures at several national healthcare and project management conferences and has been a contributing author on multiple publications related to project and configuration management. His background includes 20 years of experience in configuration management and project management, spanning across multiple government agencies and hospital systems.

Chapter 1

Introduction

> The goal of running high performance IT is to make improvement in business fundamentals and achieve high-performance business results in the long term.
>
> **– Pearl Zhu**
> *100 IT Charms: Running Versatile IT to get Digital Ready*

With healthcare organization's portfolio of software applications rapidly growing, having a defined framework for how to manage them is essential. This book will describe how utilizing a portfolio management framework throughout the application lifecycle will provide the structure to ensure that all new applications are properly evaluated and once implemented, remain relevant while continuing to meet organizational requirements.

In 2003, there were only about 31% of hospitals using electronic health record systems (EHRs), and in 2017, the number has increased to nearly 99% (Landi, 2017). Office-based physician adoption of EHRs was about 21% in 2004 and expanded to about 86% in 2017 [Health Information Technology (IT) Dashboard]. These statistics only show the adoption of EHRs, while the availability and use of specialty applications have also grown at a fast pace in the same timeframe. While an organization may have a few large "organization-wide" systems such as the EHR, lab, or radiology systems, they also have a large quantity of other clinical, administrative, and research systems. Some larger organizations now have hundreds of software applications to support and manage. While the IT staff is busy implementing new, they also have to maintain the old. Utilizing a standard, repeatable framework will help to manage the large portfolio of software applications.

Portfolio management is an organizational approach on how to manage a collection of projects and investments, such as applications. This approach provides a framework for strategic decisions related to maintaining the portfolio contents within the constraints of available resources, such as human, financial, and infrastructure. The Application Portfolio Office (APO), or the Project and Portfolio Office (PPO), is a new concept within healthcare with the focus on managing the lifecycle of all applications within the organization. This office allows for an organizational view of IT activities and investments to ensure strategic alignment with mission and goals. The purpose is to identify and eliminate redundant applications; manage changes; and evaluate the stability, quality, and sustainability of the applications within the portfolio. It keeps the focus on the organizational goals and objectives, and allocates resources based on the business value.

The lifecycle of an application begins with an idea followed by the initial request to purchase and implement the new software. There should be some form of governance where the request is reviewed and evaluated, leading to an approval decision. This is an important step that is not always in place, but since organizations have limited resources (human, financial, and other), the resources should be used on the requests with the highest priority for the organization, not the priority of the requestor or their department. Once approved, and resources are available, the initial implementation project begins. During this project, it is just as important to prepare for post-live operations and support, as it is to implement the software. Transitioning to operations and support occurs at the end of the initial implementation project and ensures the transfer of knowledge from the project team to the support team. The application will have activities related to adding new functionality and updating or upgrading throughout the operations and support phase. It remains in this phase until a disposition decision is made. Once it's useful life is over, consistent disposition practices should be followed to ensure all aspects of the application are disposed according to the approved disposition plan.

This book will follow an application through its lifecycle as well as provide basic project management principles. The chapters include a project management overview; the management of the new application request; governance; the implementation project, the transition to operations and support, operations and maintenance related to change management and other ongoing activities; and finally disposition. Below is the list of chapters and what they will cover (Figure 1.1).

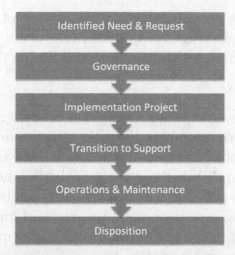

Figure 1.1   Stages of application lifecycle discussed in this book.

Project Management Overview – outlines project management principles and project management office concepts that will be used throughout the book.

New Application Request Management – describes the management and analysis of new application requests, including input from security, privacy, architecture, procurement, and others.

Governance – defines what governance is and its role, along with the type of information that is required for the committee to make educated decisions, including details on the portfolio of current projects and resource allocation and availability.

Implementation Project – describes the activities required in the project to install and implement the application while ensuring the entire system (application and infrastructure) meets regulatory requirements and properly preparations for operations and support.

Transition to Support – provides a framework for properly transitioning an application to operations and support, which includes documentation, education, and communication.

Operations and Maintenance – identifies how changes are requested, managed, and implemented after the application is live, utilizing configuration and release management or another project along with day-to-day tasks and activities that are required to ensure the application remains up to date, compliant with requirements, and the help desk is able to provide ongoing support to all users and stakeholders.

Disposition – defines the processes of a disposition plan for the application that is no longer used, compliant or relevant, and the activities that should be completed and documented during this final stage of its lifecycle.

While this book will focus on the application lifecycle, it is important to mention the software development lifecycle (SDLC) and how the two are different. SDLC is a defined process related to the development of new software or application. While there are many different definitions of the stages involved in this process, they are basically analysis, gathering of requirements and design, development, testing, and implementation. The process is cyclical and may move through the stages multiple times, such as between development and testing. An application may go through the SDLC process multiple times within its life. There is the initial development, followed by updates where new functionality is developed and implemented or the current functionality is redesigned and improved. If you are implementing a commercial-off-the-shelf (COTS) application, the vendor has already completed the development of the system prior to moving it to general availability (GA). The vast majority of these types of applications are developed to allow the organization to customize them for their unique setting or use. This process of configuring a COTS application would follow the SDLC process during the implementation project. The configuration may include anything from the values in a dropdown for clinical documentation, details for medication order, or specific layout of a report.

Before you can begin managing your portfolio of applications, you need to identify the contents. This seems fairly straightforward since it is just a list of the applications used within the organization, but it is not as easy as it may sound. It is best to start with the definition of an application. One example is a surgical solution that has separate modules for pre-op, intra-op, anesthesia, and post-op. They are all provided by one vendor and can be purchased and implemented independently, but all work together and are hosted on the same hardware. Are they one application or four? Is the application just the application or does it include the entire system, such as database(s), servers, workstations, redundancy, and backups, as well as any other environments (development, testing, or training)? Will your list of applications include those that run in the background, such as antivirus or monitoring agents? The IT leadership should be able to provide the definition so the list of applications has the right level of specificity.

Oftentimes there are multiple teams that have a list of applications based on their role in the organization. Rarely will these lists match. Gathering the separate lists and eliminating duplication will provide a good starting point. Meeting with key stakeholders from each department will provide input to what applications they currently use, no longer use, and how each meets their needs. Any application that is identified as no longer in use should move on to the disposition process, which is discussed in Chapter 8. It should not be a surprise to find applications in use that the IT department was not aware of. These are known as Shadow IT. These applications maybe something small such as running on a single workstation by a few users or larger that are hosted outside the data center and used by many. There are many reasons for Shadow IT, often it comes down to not wanting to go through the request and governance process or wanting to have complete control of "their" system.

Once there is a good list of applications, the information to track for each application depends on the purpose of the list. If it is for reporting purposes, the information to be reported should be included. If it is for support and maintenance, more information about the user groups, infrastructure, and the support documentation should be included. At a minimum, the application name, version, vendor name, departments who use it, where it is hosted (data center, department, vendor site, cloud), type of data included, and any integration should be collected. The amount of information gathered needs to be weighed between the level of detail desired and the work effort to keep the information current through any changes made during the application's lifecycle. Old, out-of-date information is worse than no information since decisions may be made on bad data.

The application list and associated information can be kept in a spreadsheet, a database, a web-based tool, or an application purchased specifically for this purpose. Something other than a spreadsheet would allow for including documents such as Service Level Agreements (SLA), Memorandums of Understanding (MOU), architecture designs, integration mapping documents, and/or help desk documentation.

The APO is responsible for managing each application as it moves through the lifecycle outlined in this book. They work with the requestors for new applications and ensure each new request is reviewed and objectively evaluated while gathering additional information so that the governance board can make an educated approval decision. If approved, APO works with the Project Management Office (PMO) to begin the implementation project once all resources are available. Once the new application is live and in use, the office facilitates the support and maintenance work until the application is ready to be disposed. The office will then facilitate the work required to dispose of the application and all its components. It is important to note that the APO has a facilitation and control role within the organization and has a dotted line reporting relationship with other teams.

Throughout this book, a case study project will be used to help describe the concepts being discussed. The initial problem is identified below.

The current hospital procedures state that after a staff nurse has pulled a medication for administration, the nurse should manually verify the right drug, the right dose, the right route, and the right time against the electronic medical record contained in the hospital's EHR. The nurse must also verify the correct patient based on existing wristband practices. Finally, the nurse charts the medication as given in the EHR. While seemingly straightforward, the number of manual processes can lead to human error, and hospital records have shown several close calls in just the past 12 months. On average, there have been 15 errors for every 5,000 medication administered. These errors could have resulted in severe adverse reactions, which makes it essential to deploy a new application that can help reduce the likelihood of these occurrences. A Bar Code Medication Administration (BCMA) system will help confirm the five patient rights of medication administration.

Chapter 2

Project Management Overview

If you fail to plan, you plan to fail.

– **Vijay Dhameliya**

Before we can evaluate the process of managing applications using a portfolio framework, it's important to understand the basic principles of project management, which in turn will drive any new implementation or modification to a successful endpoint. It's important to note that the concept of project management is not new, nor is it restricted to the world of information technology (IT) or application management. In fact, you can find principles of project management in everything from the construction of ancient monuments to the planning of your best friend's wedding. Regardless of its usage, the basic definition of a project remains the same: It is a temporary endeavor that seeks to accomplish a unique set of objectives. The two key terms here are *temporary* and *unique*. A project must have a defined start and finish date; an effort that is ongoing cannot be a project. Also, each project should have a set of objectives to create a unique product or service. Requirements cannot be open-ended, and by the end of the project, you must be able to state definitively whether your objectives were met.

Some organizations may incorrectly refer to open-ended, long-term efforts as "projects," but it's important to distinguish projects from other disciplines, such as *programs* or *product management*. A program is a series of interrelated projects that serve to meet a long-term goal. For example, a large hospital system may wish to implement barcode technology throughout its practices. This may include providing patients with scannable wristbands and affixing barcodes to virtually everything else for tracking purposes, including lab specimens, medications, supplies, devices, and food trays. Each of these components may serve the same goals of the organization, and some of the equipment and rollout processes will be identical. However, the stakeholders and applications involved with food preparation will likely be vastly different from those involved with lab specimen collection. Trying to engage such a variety of different resources, systems, and stakeholders will be challenging. Therefore, breaking each of these implementations into unique projects with a high-level program manager will likely result in a much better outcome. Any one of those projects could then generate one or more IT applications, which would need care and feeding throughout its lifecycle. To that end, some organizations elect to designate a *product* manager to one or more applications. Unlike a *project* manager (PM), who is only responsible for the unique and temporary goals of the project, a product manager oversees every aspect of an application, from new releases and features, to setting strategic objectives of how the application will evolve over the course of its lifecycle. Program managers and product managers may be engaged with multiple efforts over a long period of time, but to help establish the fundamentals of application portfolio management, this chapter will focus primarily on the role that a PM serves related to an assigned project. To that end, these are the major management areas that need to be considered throughout the course of a project:

Application/Project Portfolio Office (PPO) – is responsible for identifying and controlling the management strategy for all projects and applications from conception (when an application is being considered for implementation) through disposition (when an application is removed from the organization's portfolio). The office helps to ensure that all applications are aligned to the mission of the organization and ensures that there are standard processes in place for the management of the application, throughout its lifecycle. It would therefore be logical that any groups involved with the maintenance of these applications, including the Project Management Office (PMO) and Configuration Management Office (CMO), would report through the portfolio office to ensure that those standards are followed. The portfolio office would also provide reports to the organization's stakeholders regarding the status of any application or project.

Project Management Office (PMO) – assigns individual PMs to every approved project. The PMs would report back to the PMO manager regarding the status of their projects, including significant risks and issues. In turn, the office would help to ensure that the PMs have the appropriate resources to complete their work and escalate issues to higher levels of the organization, if necessary. The PMO also ensures that projects follow any designated process defined by the portfolio office and the organization.

Project Manager (PM) – is responsible for the day-to-day operations of an assigned project, and controls the defined scope, timeline, and budget for the work. The PM works with appropriate teams and contracts to ensure that all project resources have the materials, training, and other logistics needed to complete their workload. Typically, the PM is accountable for the success or failure of the project. A project may be successful if all stated objectives are met within the time and cost determined during project planning, even if the product itself fails to meet customer expectations.

Project Sponsor – is generally an executive-level individual that is responsible for helping to ensure the successful outcome of a project. They will be called upon to approve the scope of the project at the beginning and the closure of the project at the end. They may also have a key decision-making ability when it comes to requests for modifications during the project. Note that in larger projects, this responsibility may be delegated to a formal Change Control Board (CCB) for the project. The sponsor will also be an influencer for resolving conflicts and making other key decisions throughout the project.

Project Champion – is responsible for supporting the project and being the advocate for the adoption and acceptance of the solution. The champion role is not the same as the project sponsor or project manager. Instead, this is an informal role on the project and is held by someone who is fiercely determined to see the success of the project. In turn, this individual can provide support to the PM, sponsor, and team by navigating the politics of the organization to help sell the project to other stakeholders. Therefore, it's essential that the champion is satisfied with the progress of the project.

Project Lead – is occasionally used in large-scale projects and takes on the day-to-day project activities that are normally assigned to the PM. The lead may assist with basic deliverables, such as meeting minutes, resource alignment, and project plan updates, which allows the PM to focus on the strategic direction of the project, or focus more time on risk/issue management, earned value measurement, and project outreach and communication.

When it comes to project management, the process of how projects are managed has evolved over the years. The most traditional is considered the waterfall approach, which, as the name implies, flows from one step to another and generally does not go backward to earlier steps. However, the advancement of IT and the ability to quickly deploy modifications to requirements has offered more agile approaches, which allows customers to be highly involved in the design and construction of a project, thereby allowing their continual feedback to drive the final project outcome. Before we can examine the process involved with agile project management, let's dive into the fundamentals of the waterfall framework.

From a conceptual standpoint, the waterfall process is a logical flow, consisting of analysis, planning, designing, building, testing, and deploying. The Project Management Institute (PMI) has set global standards for project management, and in turn has encapsulated these steps into five Project Management Process Groups: (1) Initiating, (2) Planning, (3) Executing, (4) Monitoring and Controlling, and (5) Closing. According to PMI, each of these process groups contain a series of 49 unique processes that are performed at various points during the project, either periodically, continually, or at fixed intervals. Each process can become an input or an output to another process. Ultimately, PMI's guidance can be used as a toolbox, allowing each project to be tailored to the interest of the PM, PMO, or customer. Therefore, it is not necessary for this text to describe every potential component of any project. Instead, we will focus on the steps that are most applicable to successfully managing an application project.

Initiating

During *initiating*, the scope of the project is identified and confirmed with the original requestor or customer. From a formal management standpoint, the work that is completed during initiating is completed by the assigned PM. However, this is not typical in the real world, and these activities are often conducted by a member of the PMO or PPO when an initial request is being evaluated. Regardless of who completes the work, the process of scope refinement is particularly important because it will drive the requirements and ensure that the project has a defined endpoint. It may be helpful to consider the scope of the project like a contract. Once it's signed, the objectives are fixed, thereby allowing the PM and resources to plan for them accordingly. Certainly, there should be an opportunity for stakeholders and team members to request changes later in the project, but those changes are not automatic and must be analyzed for the impact on timeline, cost, resources, and other projects before they can be considered for approval.

When developing the scope of the project, the PM should compile all the appropriate stakeholders involved with the project. For context, a stakeholder can be any person, group, or entity that may be impacted by the decisions and outcomes of the project. As an example, if you were to implement a Barcode Medication Administration (BCMA) system within a hospital, your stakeholders would certainly include patients, nursing staff, and pharmacists, but there are others as well. The PM should include the system vendor, senior hospital leadership, hospital communication and patient outreach offices, and even the suppliers of the equipment to be deployed (scanners, printers, labels). The stakeholders in the IT department may be even more impacted by this project. The IT stakeholders could include the system administrators that need to install and configure servers for the application, the customer/user support teams that need to install and support the scanners and printers, the testers that create testing plans based on the project requirements, and the trainers that need to develop electronic and paper-based materials for initial and ongoing training. If you take some time to think about the stakeholders, your list could be even more expansive, and if you ask these groups "who else" may need to be included, it may seem that your list will never end. Managing all the different groups and people can be overwhelming, so planning the communication strategy early in the project is critical. Oftentimes, a Stakeholder Register can be a helpful way to organize these groups and set appropriate expectations. Table 2.1 demonstrates how a PM can simplify the stakeholder management.

Once the stakeholders are identified and appropriately engaged in the project, the scope can be integrated into a formal project charter document. Although the charter is generally of high level and does not identify every requirement of the project, it serves an important purpose to formally authorize the PM's activities, as well as the project itself. Some of the key components of the project charter include: (1) Measurable objectives and key deliverables that, when completed or canceled, will signal the termination of the project; (2) Justification for why the project and/or application is needed; (3) Initial list of risks, assumptions, and constraints that could impact the project; and (4) The names of key personnel, including the PM, project sponsor, and other parties that have a role in authorizing the project. Once the charter has been approved, the project can move into the planning process. From this point until the project is closed, the PM is responsible

Table 2.1 Stakeholder Management Example

Stakeholder	Contact	Role	Interest (H/M/L)	Influence (H/M/L)	Expectations
Mike S.	mikes@ hosp.com	Sponsor	H	H	Weekly update
Pamela B.	pamelab@ hosp.com	Vendor	H	M	As needed
James H.	jamesh@ hosp.com	Sys Admin	L	M	Build requirements
Angela M.	angelam@ hosp.com	Tester	M	M	Config requirements
Darryl P.	darrylp@ hosp.com	Trainer	H	L	Daily check-in

for ensuring all the activities conducted during the project follow a standard procedure, defined by an organization's PMO.

Planning

The *planning* process should be carefully and thoroughly documented through a formal project management plan, which will specify every aspect as to how the project will be managed. The charter document that was created earlier will provide the most immediate guidance for the development of detailed requirements. In a typical waterfall approach, requirements would be collected upfront, approved, and built according to their specifications. A project that's managed in a more agile approach allows requirements to be collected in an iterative fashion, allowing customers to provide feedback as a product is being built or configured. In either case, the requirements must adhere to the original scope and charter of the project and should only be used to refine the specific work that will be done to meet those high-level objectives. When new products are being purchased, the requirements and expectations that were defined in the original Statement of Work (SOW) can be a good source to define the scope and initial set of requirements for the project.

The process of gathering requirements can be handed off to a system or business analyst, who has a skill set of eliciting requirements from customers and stakeholders. Think about the process you would use to determine the requirements for a new car. Perhaps you may already know the type of car you want (sedan, sport utility, truck, or minivan), as well as the color and basic features like backup cameras and blind spot monitoring. You will also have to contend with regulatory requirements on the car, like air bags, turn signals, and emissions regulations. However, there may be other features that you need but may not even consider upfront, incorrectly assuming that every car must have those options, such as automatic transmission and cruise control. To that end, most people work with a salesperson, who can help explain available options and communicate the impact of those decisions on the cost and timeline of receiving a car with those specifications. In a similar way, even applications that are purchased as commercial off-the-shelf (COTS) systems still have some level of unique configuration that needs to occur before the system is production-ready for the given organization. The analyst should be able to ask questions to the customer and stakeholders to determine what specific features are needed at the point of go live. The customer should also understand that until those requirements are approved, no work will begin. Likewise, once the requirements are documented and approved, no changes can be made without a full review and approval of the impacts of those modifications.

Upon approval of the project requirements, the PM will be able to work with appropriate stakeholders to develop a formal project timeline, including the resources and funding needed for each part of the project. This is most often completed using a Work Breakdown Structure (WBS), which divides the project deliverables and requirements into manageable work packages. In other words, the objectives should be translated into specific, measurable, and time-specific tasks that can be assigned to an individual on the project team. Once completed, the PM will use that document to control the project activities and clearly identify what is required from every resource at every step of the system implementation. Breaking down or "decomposing" a project can be more challenging that it may seem, especially because the PM is not necessarily the subject matter expert on the work that is being completed.

Let's say that you have a project to build a new wing of a hospital, and one of your objectives is to construct ten new patient rooms. You could break that objective into ten work packages for each patient room, but that would not provide sufficient detail. To build out one room, you would need to consider the construction crew, electricians, plumbers, painters, and other roles, and if you only had a single task to monitor all of that work, it would be almost impossible to control the status of the project. Likewise,

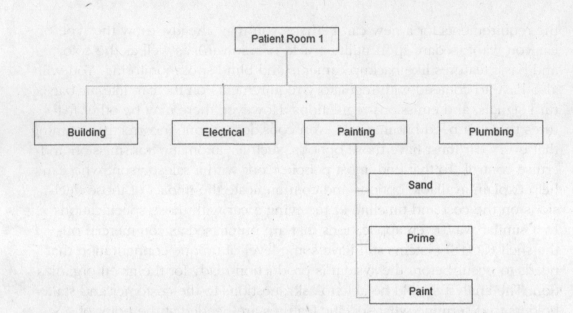

Figure 2.1   WBS diagram.

it's not advisable to break out a project too specifically, either. If you took the work of the painters, you could break that out into sanding, priming, and painting. From there, you could replicate those tasks to each wall of the room, and from there to each brushstroke. Although you may be able to specifically pinpoint exactly where you are in the project, the workload to maintain such a plan would not provide any real benefit. Every project is unique, and there is no single answer to how detailed a project plan should be. However, a common measurement is to ensure that work package is no longer than 80 hours in length and no shorter than 8 hours. Once the work packages are identified, they can be illustrated in a WBS diagram, as shown in Figure 2.1.

Identifying the work packages to include in the plan is a team effort. One methodology is to perform a sticky-note meeting early in the project with all appropriate stakeholders. During that meeting, the PM can review the objectives for the project and invite the attendees to use sticky notes to document specific tasks that they would need to accomplish to meet a stated requirement. The notes can be collected and arranged in a group setting to quickly organize some of the project work that would eventually become part of the WBS. Other methods include using project templates from similar requests and reviewing lessons learned from prior implementations. Once the tasks are identified and organized, there are a few additional attributes that should be added:

Dependencies – are the constraints added to each task. In other words, a task may not be able to start or finish until certain criteria are met. For example, before the painters can paint the walls of the new patient rooms, the builders need to install the walls. Although this is an obvious, inherent trait, documenting these dependencies helps to define the critical path of the project. The critical path is the shortest possible duration of a project, driven by each task that has a dependency on another. If the builders finish their work late, the painters will start late, and the end date of the project could be impacted. Other dependencies could be related to external factors, such as the availability and delivery of a key product or resource that is needed for another task. It's therefore important for the PM to be aware of these dependencies and how they might impact the project.

Resources – are the people that will be assigned to complete the work. By documenting both the resource and work hours of tasks, the PM can have a better understanding of potential resource conflicts and drive more realistic timelines. For example, the PM may have a team assigned to a project task, but that team may only be able to spend 25% of their time working on the project, due to their other day-to-day duties. In factoring resource availability, a task that is designed to take 40 hours may actually take a full month to complete. This becomes a key driver to the overall project timeline.

Cost – is the financial aspect of any given task. At a minimum, every task typically involves human workers with unique salary requirements. Additionally, some tasks may include the procurement of products or other resources. By including the cost of each task, the PM can generate a total cost for the project and monitor associated funding throughout its lifecycle.

Once the WBS is finalized and documented into a project workplan, along with the appropriate inputs from the scope, charter, and system requirements, the PM can identify a reasonable expectation of the potential go-live date and predicted cost of the project. The final documentation should be signed by the project sponsor, and upon signoff, those documents form a baseline for the project. Should any changes be requested and approved in the future, the PM will need to create a new project baseline for the scope, schedule, and cost.

During project planning, the PM should start to identify the potential project risks. Optimally, every project within an organization's portfolio would take the same approach to managing risk on a given project, but that process should still be tailored to each project based on its size, complexity, and visibility. Although the term risk can throw up multiple red flags for those in a management role, risk identification and management are vital components of project management, as it allows the team to proactively plan for potential issues later in the project, even to the point of avoiding certain risks altogether. It's important to remember that risks are only a possibility, not a definite, and not all risks are negative. For those working in the healthcare industry, for example, there is always a risk of additional regulation or government-mandated policies and practices that could impact day-to-day operations. However, sometimes those policy changes are intended to remove red tape or provide financial incentives for certain technology improvements, which are typically positive for the organization(s) that are impacted. Regardless of the type of risk, it's important for the PM to track and monitor them. Some of the criteria that should be tracked with each risk include the probability of whether it will occur, and if it does, what the impact of that risk would be. This helps categorize risks that need the most stringent planning and monitoring. One common method to track risks is via a Risk Register (see example in Table 2.2).

Note that the process of identifying risk is not solely the responsibility of the PM. In fact, the PM should never be considered the subject matter expert on any new product or service. Instead, every stakeholder should take an active role in helping to identify potential risks. From there, the PM can assist with tracking and monitoring those risks.

The project planning process goes beyond just the planning for the product or service that will be delivered at the end of the project. The PM also

Table 2.2 Risk Register Example

Risk	Probability	Impact	Mitigation	Owner
Resources will be diverted to higher-priority project	Medium	Medium	Prepare short-term contractual staff	PM
Coding and configuration from similar system cannot be reused	Low	High	Evaluate compatibility of system databases	DBA
Work scheduled during winter with possible snow-related closures	Medium	Low	Ensure staff have ability to work remotely	PM

needs to plan and document how the project itself will be managed. Oftentimes, templates provided by the PMO can be repurposed or even duplicated across similar projects. However, the PM must still ensure that those processes are in alignment with his or her assigned project, while still falling in line with the expectations dictated by the PMO and PPO. The following checklist can be used to help confirm that the minimum documentation has been completed, and the project is ready to move forward:

■ The scope and objectives of the project are identified and confirmed
■ High-level requirements are documented
■ A detailed project workplan is created with associated dependencies and durations
■ Human resources have been requested to complete the project tasks
■ The total estimated cost of the project is known, and a budget is confirmed
■ Stakeholders are identified, and a plan for engagement is documented
■ Known risks are defined, reviewed, and communicated
■ The project scope, plan, and resources are approved by a sponsor

Execution

Project *execution* refers to the actual process of completing the work defined in the approved scope and workplan. It is important to reiterate that no work should begin against the plan until the project is approved, and no work should be completed outside of the scope of that work without additional reviews and approvals. It is the PM's responsibility to ensure that all stakeholders and team members are aware of that requirement. It is also during this phase that the PM is responsible for directing, monitoring, and controlling all project work in accordance to the documents created during project planning. Since execution involves all the work required to meet the defined scope and objectives, there are several activities that the PM can do to help manage the workload.

Resource Management – defines how project resources are acquired and used throughout the project. This is particularly important for multisite hospitals, where resources can be geographically scattered across a wide area. Additionally, if the hospital does not have the appropriate IT department or related skill sets to complete the project, there may be a need to outsource those roles. PMs that work in an environment that is centralized and small in scale may already have staff available in-house. However, even in those situations, the managers of respective teams will want to know what work will be required of their team members and how long it will take.

Developing a successful project team requires a comprehensive knowledge of the skill sets of the members of the team, the culture of the organization, and the availability of each resource. Understanding the most effective communication strategy of the team is essential. Often, facilitating a weekly team meeting can be an effective way of ensuring everyone is on par with expectations and project status. However, projects that have higher visibility or criticality to the organization may require more routine check-ins. To ensure these meetings are constructive, the focus should stay in line with a standing agenda, typically involving the review of active and upcoming tasks, current issues, and potential risks. The outcome of these meetings should be documented and disseminated to team members and appropriate stakeholders in a timely manner to help ensure that meeting discussions were consistently understood by all attendees. It's also useful for the PM to maintain logs for action items (tasks occurring within the scope of the project but not necessarily included as part of the project workplan) and decisions (confirmed directionality by sponsors or managers). Advancements in technology have offered the ability for staff to attend meetings in a virtual manner through conference calls and remote screen sharing. While this allows greater flexibility for staff scheduling, it also requires additional discipline from the team and greater control by the PM to keep the team members engaged in the project.

Issue Management – is similar to risk management, although it addresses how actual incidents will be managed during the project. An active project issue indicates that there is some situation that is having an impact on the project's progression. Sometimes, issues may generate from documented risks, requiring the implementation of stated mitigation strategies. In other cases, issues may occur as a result of unknown risks, testing occurrences, or stakeholder feedback. It's important for the PM to document issues as thoroughly as possible and indicate the severity and impact of that issue on the project. Each issue should be assigned to a team member, and once resolved, the process that was used to address the issue should be fully documented before the issue is closed. In many cases in IT, an issue may present itself in a development environment months before the application is moved to production. If the issue were to recur later, the team can immediately refer back to the original documentation to determine how to rectify the situation. It's helpful for the PM to develop an issue log to track each issue on the project – as shown in the example in Table 2.3.

Table 2.3 Issue Log Example

Issue	Priority	Impact	Action Plan/Resolution	Owner
James H. will be on unexpected leave for 3 months	Medium	High	Identify tasks that can be transitioned to other staff or delayed	PM
System performance is extremely poor	High	Medium	Increase hardware specifications	Sys Admin
Spelling issues reported in the application	Low	Low	Document all errors and report to vendor	Tester

All issues should be closed by the end of the project, either through their resolution or by assignment of follow-up actions through separate processes.

Procurement Management – includes the acquisition of any supplies or services that will occur during the project. Although some organizations keep procurement actions separate from the IT or project team, it's possible that the contracting officer or representative will be included as a team member on the project, or the sponsor may expect any costs associated with procurement actions to be managed through the project. In that case, the PM should be aware of the major tasks associated with procurement and determine what level of tracking will be necessary from the project standpoint. Even in situations where the PM may not directly manage procurement actions, he or she may be called upon to provide feedback on contractor performance and hours worked. Additionally, most contracts have scheduled deliverables that must be met on a timely basis, and the PM may need to report on the completion status of those items. In some cases, deliverables have financial incentives associated with their quality and/or timeliness, which makes the management of those deliverables that much more important.

In the IT industry, there is an increasing trend for software applications to be sold as Software as a Service (SaaS), where the vendor will provide all responsibility to host and update the application remotely. In turn, this will require the project to generate Service Level Agreements (SLAs), Memorandums of Understanding (MOUs), and other documentation to ensure the security and privacy of data that is hosted outside of the customer's organization.

In addition to managing procurement activities, the PM should control the costs of the project against the defined project baseline.

There are many factors that can contribute to fluctuations in cost, including internal factors, such as the loss of a project resource, and external factors, such as inclement weather, which could hamper the ability for staff to complete their assigned work. Of course, these factors can also impact the schedule of the project. As project activities occur, the PM will find that some tasks take longer to complete, while others may be finished sooner than expected. Since it's rare for a project to follow the precise day-by-day estimates, it's difficult to determine simply by cost or time alone whether the project is ahead or behind schedule or budget. One common method of tracking these variances is through Earned Value Management (EVM). EVM allows the PM to calculate the earned value of work performed and thereby determine the actual status of the project. For example, a 1-year project with a budget of $1 million may have used 75% of the budget within 2 months. Initially, that may seem that the project is far over budget, but if the majority of the cost was for equipment, scheduled to be purchased within the first quarter of the project, it's possible that the project is actually on target or even ahead of the projected budget for the amount of work performed.

Change Management – refers to determining how any potential change in the project objectives or requirements will be handled. Despite the efforts of the PM, sponsor, and analyst, there's always a possibility that there will be a need to modify something that was previously approved, especially for complex and long-term projects. One of the most familiar types of changes are those associated with undocumented or unrealized requirements. However, changes could also be driven based on newly identified risks or issues, new laws or regulations, or defects that are identified during testing. Preventing any type of change would generally be considered as unacceptable as accepting every type of change. If a PM allows any change to the project scope, workplan, or requirements, it would constitute scope creep, which is never acceptable on any project. A change that occurs after appropriate approvals is not considered to be scope creep, as it would be an approved modification to the original project baseline.

The PM must plan for how changes will be submitted, evaluated, and decided upon. At a minimum, this should entail a formal impact analysis, including an evaluation of how the change would affect resources, cost, time, scope, and other projects. It's also helpful to include an analysis of alternate options. Ultimately, no action should be taken on the requested change(s) until a decision is reached by either the project sponsor or a CCB. Decisions can range from acceptance to deferment or outright denial.

If a change is accepted, the PM should ensure that all team members and appropriate stakeholders are aware of the modification, and any associated project documentation should be updated. Changes could have a permanent effect on the project requirements, cost, timeline, and resources, so the PM must make appropriate updates to those project components and create a new baseline. Given the impact that change can have on a project, this text will provide a much deeper dive with examples in Chapter 5.

Quality Management – refers to the ability of a product or service to meet the original requirements of the customer. While this may seem like an obvious nod to customer service, ensuring quality is mutually beneficial to the project, as it reduces the potential of rework, and increases the likelihood of future work and projects with the customer. Since every project is unique, the requirements for how much assurance is placed on quality will vary, as well. Some organizations may see quality as a cornerstone of their business practices and will integrate quality processes throughout. An example of this would be using Six Sigma practices, which is the concept of developing processes that will result in products or services that have extremely low numbers of defects. Although this is most commonly used in the manufacturing industry, the same concept can be applied to the healthcare industry. For example, a hospital may wish to reduce emergency room wait times or increase the turnaround time for insurance claim reimbursement. If quality is integrated into the culture of the organization, this becomes the foundation for successful quality management on a project, as well.

Even if quality management is not a key metric for an organization, assuring quality is still a critical component to project management. Some of the methods a PM may wish to employ to help ensure products and services meet expectations can include

- Deploying a variety of internal testing techniques before releasing anything to the customer. Testing should be planned early in the project and can include
  - Unit Testing – is the most independent level of testing, typically performed on a self-contained unit level to ensure that a single requirement is met.
  - Function/Integration Testing – verifies that the requirement functions as designed with other existing processes or with other stated requirements.
  - Regression Testing – checks existing functionality to verify that no new bugs or issues have been created as a result of a change

- – Load Testing – mimics varying levels of concurrent user access on a system to evaluate performance
- – Acceptance Testing – verifies that the entire package of changes being implemented with the project meet the stated objectives
- ■ Creating automated testing and validation criteria. It's possible that some forms of validation can be completed via regular reporting. There are also software tools available that can virtually mimic real-life scenarios, such as varying levels of user load on a system.
- ■ Adding the customer or end user to the project team to assist with acceptance and validation. This can be accomplished through planned user acceptance testing, pilot deployments, and early adopters. It is not advisable to include the customer until at least internal testing is complete, as there is only one opportunity to make a first impression, and releasing a product of poor initial quality will not reflect well on the entire project. However, agile approaches to project management may include more routine reviews with the customer, as they are considered to be partners in the development of the new system or application.
- ■ Providing demonstrations, road shows, and town halls to collect feedback from a wider audience.

It may initially seem as though adding more stakeholders to the review process may make for an even higher-quality product, but this may not always be the case. In fact, as a product is demonstrated to a wider group of people, there will be more ideas for features and requirements that were never part of the scope of the project, which will increase the likelihood of change requests or scope creep. A product that meets all the stated requirements but has limited features would be considered high quality and low grade. From a PM standpoint, the grade of the product or service is not of concern, as that determination is made by the customer when they initially provided their requirements for the project. However, the quality of the product or service in meeting the original objectives is critical to the success of any project.

Management Reviews – are points in the project where the PM and appropriate stakeholders and sponsors review work completed to that point. Generally, for the project to move forward, there must be a review of certain project documentation and an agreement that the project should continue progressing towards its stated objectives. This process provides assurance to the PM, team members, and stakeholders alike that the project is on track, and any risks and issues are clearly identified and communicated.

The best practice for management reviews is for them to take place at specific, designated intervals of the project. Each review should include specific deliverables and documentation to justify that the project has reached a certain threshold. For example, if you were implementing new hospital software, the PM may plan for a review (1) When the scope, requirements, and workplan are baselined and work is ready to start; (2) When the design of the system is completed and coding/configuration is ready to start; (3) When internal testing is complete and initial handoff to the customer can start; and (4) When the entire system has been validated and is ready for production use. Notice that these review points take place just prior to significant milestones on the project. This provides the sponsor or other management bodies with the opportunity to make strategic decisions on the direction of the project. Their approval to move forward is an indication that all prior work has been completed to their satisfaction. Likewise, it allows them to provide a temporary or permanent halt in the project if objectives are not being met. It is not advisable for the PM to enter a management review if there are still outstanding issues or action items associated with work completed to that point.

During a management review, the PM should provide key project status documentation to assist the decision maker, including

- A summary of work accomplished to that point
- A review of the earned value of the work accomplished
- Any risks involved with moving the project forward past the review phase
- The planned work to be accomplished until the next management review

Activation Planning – is one of the final steps taken in a project prior to releasing the product or service to customers. Activation planning involves two key steps: (1) Preparing the internal project team for activities associated with bringing a system live and (2) Preparing the external stakeholders for changes associated with the project's activation. The former may seem less intensive, since the project team has been working toward these common goals since day 1, but there is still a lot of planning to consider to keep things running smoothly.

Throughout the course of a project, the PM and project team have generally had some level of flexibility with regard to time. If someone was coding a new system feature and it wasn't working correctly, they could always take a break, go home, get some rest, and come back to tackle the issue with a fresh mind the next day. However, this will not be feasible amid a new system implementation where hours and minutes matter. The PM must take responsibility to ensure that the activation team has what they need to complete their work quickly and should prepare for alternate outcomes. Even the physical location of the project team will matter. If staff will be physically scattered across a wide area during the activation, how will communication be most effective? If staff will be centrally located, does that area have appropriate power, network, and other connections? If the work is being performed off-hours, the PM may even need to consider the availability of the area's heating and cooling systems, which may automatically shut down overnight, as well as food and drinks for activations that are expected to take several hours to complete, when normal restaurants and convenience stores may be closed.

To help plan for the activities that will take place during the activation, the PM may wish to conduct another sticky-note style meeting. This time the focus will be significantly narrower than the 80-to-8-hour guideline that was employed during the development of the project's WBS. Instead, the PM should be aware of what each person needs to do on a minute-by-minute basis and track that information on a checklist. This is particularly important in hospital settings, where even a few minutes' delay in the availability of a system could lead to serious complications for a patient. Project team members should be encouraged to review their past work, meeting minutes, and other documentation to help identify the tasks that need to be performed.

To help plan out the duration of tasks, it may be beneficial for the PM to conduct a mock activation in a development environment that does not impact the end user. The mock activation should be treated as if it were a production activation, with all applicable staff engaged throughout the mock's duration. This process not only serves as a rehearsal for the team members but also provides the PM with additional assurances that the checklist's tasks, durations, and resources are accurate. In turn, this will provide guidance on communication to end users about potential system interruptions on the day of production activation.

In addition to planning out internal team processes, the PM must also plan how stakeholders are engaged throughout the go live. At a minimum, this would involve communication about any downtime. If the hospital has had a long period of time since the last planned or unplanned down, the PM may want to engage with nurse managers and service providers to ensure that staff are well versed in downtime procedures and practices. Department and hospital leadership should also be engaged to help determine a timeframe that is least impactful to staff and patients. Often, this may involve avoiding changes in shift and requiring off-hours or weekend support.

The PM should also consider ancillary staff that may be needed beyond the core project team. This could include user support and helpdesk staff, who may have an influx of calls during and immediately after the activation. Setting expectations and preparing these teams with scripts and knowledge of the changes being implemented with the project is crucial for success. Additionally, project activations that are expected to take significant time to complete may require backup or secondary resources to relieve the core project team. It's always possible that a key member of the project team will become ill or otherwise be unable to perform their duties, and having a last-minute delay of a major activation on account of one person is likely not going to be acceptable to leadership. By reviewing and rereviewing project activation activities ahead of time and anticipating any and all possible risks will result in a much smoother go live for all parties involved.

Closing

Once all the objectives have been met, the project can begin *closing* activities. This is the final phase of the project and ensures all deliverables and documents are properly archived, and resources and contractors are released from the project. However, there are a few more project activities that the PM should complete during closing.

Support expectations must be clearly communicated to customers and stakeholders. Throughout the duration of the project, the PM has been the ringleader, but once the project is closed, the PM should optimally have no ongoing association with that product or service. Instead, customers should be directed to a product owner or support center for future support. However, it would not be unreasonable for the PM and project team to remain engaged for 2–4 weeks after the go live to capture and quickly follow-up on issues. This time period can also be used to ensure that ongoing support mechanisms are working properly, and staff have the information they need to manage the system. Chapter 6 of this book will provide a clear outline to successfully transition a project to ongoing operations.

Project closing also provides an opportunity for the team to reflect on all work performed during the project and document highlights in a lessons learned document. The PM should collect and organize lessons learned for reference on future projects. Although it's typically easier to think of the things that did not go as expected, the emphasis should always be on promoting positive outcomes. That doesn't necessarily mean that there aren't things that can be done better in the future, but the PM should steer the team away from finger-pointing or shifting blame, as the goal should be for even better outcomes on the next project. Optimally, lessons are not solely collected at the conclusion of the project, as there is an opportunity to obtain more precise and useful feedback throughout the project duration. In fact, the PM may even be able to make on-the-spot adjustments to the active project if feedback is encouraged and collected throughout. Note that not all staff may be comfortable speaking out in a formal lessons learned meeting, so the PM should be careful to gather input in a variety of formats, including surveys, interviews, and even social media platforms and wikis. Above all, it's essential that lessons are not collected merely to meet an objective of the PMO, but they should be documented in a central database for all future projects and managers to reference.

In addition to documenting lessons learned, the PM should ensure that all project activities are complete and objectives are met. Every task that was identified in the WBS should be finished, and if there is anything outstanding, the project cannot be closed without a project scope change request to formally remove that item from the scope of work. If one of those tasks or deliverables is still needed but could be completed outside the context of the project, the PM should check if the organization has any tracking mechanisms, perhaps in the configuration management office or support desk ticketing systems. If so, the handoff to those systems can be documented with a tracking number and referenced in the project closeout documentation. Likewise, the project should not be closed if there are outstanding issues or risks in the project. Outstanding items like these should be closed or reassigned to a support team that is not directly affiliated with the project.

Any documents that were created during the project should be archived in accordance with the expectations of the organization or the PMO, which may include both physical and electronic copies of signed documents. If there are any pending payments due to contractors or vendors as a result of the project, those should be completed before the PM exits. In addition, if there is any additional training that is due to end users, support teams, or other staff, that should also be completed. Finally, after all work is completed, the PM should write up an after-action report or other project closing notice for final signoff by the project sponsor. Once approved to close, the team and PM can be formally released. Of course, sometime in the course of these activities, don't forget to celebrate the accomplishments of the project and recognize staff that went the extra mile to ensure the project's success.

Much of what has been reviewed so far has focused on a traditional waterfall approach to project management. However, before we move on to the next chapter, we'll take a moment to explore some of the traits associated with agile project management and how that may differ from some of the concepts reviewed so far. In general, the goals of both waterfall and agile are the same: To accomplish a unique set of objectives within a specified budget and timeframe. The most significant difference is how PMs manage the efforts to accomplish those goals.

An agile framework takes the traditional fixed-and-firm scope and expects that there will be modifications to the design of a product during the course of a project. Instead of focusing on solutions that are saturated with user requirements, the goal is to meet objectives faster, while still satisfying the overall needs of the end user. Consider this: If you are a lab tech and you wanted a better process for managing specimens, you may be able to think of a few dozen requirements that would make for an optimal system. However, perhaps a couple of those requirements are extremely difficult for the project team to meet and will drive up the cost and timeline of the entire project. And for what it's worth, you would rather have some system in place sooner that meets most of the requirements, rather than a robust system that could take months or years to implement. This is the key driver of agile methodologies – to identify items that will satisfy customers, while cutting out the waste of requirements that may only be "nice to have."

Adapting to an agile mindset requires staff to be open and collaborative with their customers. Rather than waiting until a project is finalized before presenting anything to the end user, the customer effectively becomes part of the project team and is crucial to the iterative effort of creating a product or service that meets the fundamental objectives of the project. Of course, this does require the PM and team to set appropriate expectations with the customer. A product that is only demonstrated in strawman or framework perspectives may not elicit excitement to the customer, but it will help drive more precise and necessary requirements as the build progresses. Also, since products are created in an iterative manner, the initial financial investment in the project can be smaller.

Agile project management puts the project team members and developers at the front and center of the work effort. Instead of working in a back room trying to decipher requirements created by the PM and sponsor, they work in tandem with the customer to deliver products that directly meet their needs. The requirement of "the system shall" translates into a user story that is more generic, along the lines of "As a [role in organization], I want a feature than can [do something] so that I can [perform specific work better]." Once the developer has a better understanding of who the user is and what they are trying to accomplish, they can be more creative in designing a system within the capacity of what technology can deliver. From there, the project team member and customer can work on appropriate acceptance criteria. These become incorporated into the fundamental product design that, when met, will satisfy the needs of the user story. Of course, the PM still needs to manage the overall workflow and ensure that each changing requirement is still within the originally approved scope and objectives.

You may now start to consider why a PM would ever choose to complete a project using the waterfall approach, since agile seems so much more streamlined and focused on the customer's needs. This is precisely why many organizations have begun to adopt agile methodologies to begin with. However, notice that the focus is on the development of new IT solutions. Even if a project uses a lean agile approach, there is still considerable cost involved with the development of a new system, plus the ongoing feeding and maintenance required to adhere to security and privacy considerations, new laws and regulations, and ongoing customer requests for enhancements. To that end, it may not always be appropriate to develop customized software solutions, especially if there are COTS software products that are already available and can meet most of the customer's needs. The companies that create these software solutions want to create a one-size-fits-all application to help streamline their own operations and maintenance of the product. Increasingly, these products allow for a certain amount of customization by the hospital, but those changes are handled at a software-configuration level, rather than a software-creation level. Therefore, there is still a need for traditional project management practices for the deployment and configuration of these commercial software products.

Having covered the fundamentals of project management, the next chapters will walk through the entire lifecycle of application management, from concept through implementation and maintenance, and finally to disposition of the product. All of these processes start with a single customer idea.

Chapter 3

New Application Request Management

If you want something new, you have to stop doing something old.

– Peter Drucker

Project request management is the concept of controlling how new projects and ideas for applications are brought forward for potential implementation. While it may seem like a straightforward process (create a form, then have the customer fill out said form), there are several considerations an organization should make when developing a process for new requests that are comprehensive, yet straightforward. To start, it's important to get over the idea that new requests are a bad thing. After all, accepting any type of request into the pipeline could lead an organization astray from its core mission, while information technology (IT) staff are overwhelmed with the amount of work already on their plates. Sometimes it's just easier to let individual hospital department do whatever they want. If the head of the nutrition department saw a really amazing new product at a trade show that could significantly speed up delivery of food to patients, why not let them go ahead with the purchase and implementation, especially if the vendor promises to do all the heavy lifting – even hosting it on their own servers in the cloud? It would save the IT department a lot of work, and in the grand scheme of things, it's probably not going to impact anyone else, right?

The concept of purchasing, developing, implementing, or using an IT product without involving the organization's IT department is known as "Shadow IT," and as almost any IT professional will tell you, shadow IT is a dangerous place for any organization, especially in healthcare. When products are selected or implemented without going through a formal request, governance, and management process, the organization could be at an even greater risk than not implementing the life-and-cost-saving solution to begin with. What's the big deal? Consider the following risks of not knowing about new IT initiatives:

- **Unapproved or illegal procurements:** When making a purchase for any piece of software, from a massive new electronic health record (EHR) to a simple plug-and-play single-user application, you are entering into a legally binding agreement. Do you really read every word of all those end user licensing agreements when installing software? And if you do, do you understand what you are agreeing to? Elevate that to the level of an organization, and your customers could be committing the company to situations that are not in alignment with policy, or at worst, criminal.

- **Last-minute and unplanned resource requests:** Let's face it – you have a limited number of people and an even greater list of customers to please. Even if you have an excellent set of dedicated staff, if requests for support arrive unplanned or unannounced, it can be jarring, confusing, and ultimately distracting from the core goals you are trying to accomplish. And are you even able to say "no"? If a customer has already spent several thousand dollars on a new IT solution and committed the organization to the implementation of the product within a set timeline and if you have no formal request management process, then there is little that you can other than begrudgingly comply.

- **Escalating costs:** Poor planning for new IT acquisitions lead not only to staff shifting their priorities, but there's a good possibility of rework and revisions, since the final requirements were not fully defined upfront.

- **Duplicate IT solutions:** This is particularly the case for large, multihospital organizations. Vendors love selling their products, but they would be even happier to sell you multiple expensive licenses across various isolated departments, instead of a single enterprise-level agreement. Having the same product implemented independently instead of house-wide leads to duplicative efforts from everyone, and of course, lots of wasted money.

- **Solutions that are not in line with organization's objectives:** Consider the tired tagline, "Is it good for the company?" There is a bit of importance to that question. If staff are working on IT solutions that do not contribute to the mission of the organization, whether it's patient safety or profits, is it really worth doing?

■ **Unknown or uncontrolled data flows:** Integration and interoperability are key to the smooth flow of information in a hospital, and if data is flowing to places that you do not expect (or may not control), there is a real risk of loss or compromised data. If that data includes patient information, there could even be significant legal and financial impacts. Ensuring that every project request undergoes an architectural review to determine any potential data flows can help mitigate this risk.

■ **Heightened risks of security/privacy issues:** Even if none of the other risks convince you and your leadership about the importance of proper request management, this one should. Healthcare organizations are the stewards of a plethora of information about their patients, and much of that data is used hour-by-hour, minute-by-minute to make life-altering decisions. Can you trust that the data in your system hasn't been manipulated by an outside party? What would happen if all, or even a subset, of your patients' data was released to the public? Or what if you lost even a few precious days' worth of information due to a ransomware attack? These situations are real, and they happen daily. If you don't have control of every IT application in your portfolio, there is a real possibility that your hospital leadership will be on every news network, trying to apologize and explain how X or Y could possibly happen.

■ **Wasted time:** Whether it's time spent developing or purchasing unnecessary applications, or it's time spent undoing a complex portfolio of applications down the line, time is always money, and wasting it can never be acceptable.

■ **Postlive support expectations are not met:** If an application does not follow an approved process for implementation, there likely will not be appropriate processes followed for postlive support, either. The application may lack standard configuration and change management practices, which will increase the amount of shadow IT in the future, as new change requests will not be documented, approved, or tested according to any formal procedures implemented by the organization. In turn, this can cause unexpected downtimes, uncommunicated changes, and unplanned risk to the data in the system. Additionally, since the application is not known to the IT department, there will be no help desk or other centralized expertise to provide support as issues arise.

■ **Demoralized IT department:** Employees want to feel valued, and they want to feel that their work is worthwhile and contributing to the success of the company. If your organization is facing a complicated influx of seemingly random application implementations, it will be increasingly difficult to demonstrate that you are headed in a planned, controlled direction. At first, staff will just do what they are told to do, but eventually, without a common vision where all applications support the organization's mission, the best people in your team will find more organized work elsewhere.

Clearly, shadow IT can lead to some severe complications for an organization, so the next step is to determine how to bring this work out into the limelight and out of the shadows. You will want to develop a request management process that is simple and fair, easy to understand, and does not tie up day-to-day workload with significant red tape. It's important to remember that regardless of how well you conduct your rollout, people may initially reject it. After all, they were used to getting almost anything they wanted in the past, and now they need to get in line with everyone else. To make this successful, you will need to be certain that you have a plan that has received full endorsement from your organization's top leadership, as well as the key influencers in various departments. Complaints from naysayers will eventually trickle up to these groups, and you must ensure that they will have your back in defending the process. You do not have a second chance at a first impression, so this chapter will provide the necessary guidance to create a strong and convincing plan.

The first step in developing any plan to present to leadership is to determine what the focus point needs to be. What are the biggest pain points the organization is currently facing? Perhaps you could gather feedback from surveys and data from past application implementations, especially those that did not go according to plan. Some key areas of focus to convince your leadership of the need for formal request management include

- **Quality of service:** Certainly, a well-executed plan is better than no plan at all, but how else will request management benefit the organization from a quality standpoint? Having more eyes on a given application while there is still an opportunity to provide input to requirements will allow you to ensure that new systems are meeting more global needs for both the present and future states of the organization.
- **Cost savings:** Are there examples in the organization where you have duplicate solutions or multiple applications that are serving similar needs? Perhaps a formal request process could help identify those well before procurement actions are finalized.

- **Streamlined services:** How can the services provided by the IT department be more accessible and efficient? Are customers getting the input they need throughout an implementation process? A new request process could include the tracking of requests and allowing requestors to see where their ideas are in the overall pipeline.
- **Fair process:** In order to be successful, you need to ensure that everyone's requests will be handled in a similar fashion. If you have ever gambled in a casino or state lotto drawing, you know that there is a good chance that you will come out on the losing end of the deal, but you also know that you have just as much a shot of getting the jackpot as everyone else, and that's a key reason that industry has been so successful. Likewise, every request should follow the same process for collection and evaluation, and there should be no unnecessary influence from favoritism, politics, or even the IT department. That's right; the IT department needs to be removed from the request management process. Sure, IT has strong, legitimate opinions on new applications, but the management of new requests must be business-driven. IT certainly deserves a seat at the table, but accepting or evaluating new requests should not be part of their responsibility. At a high level, the responsibility of IT is to provide services and fulfill requirements. For healthcare organizations in particular, IT should not be driving those services or requirements. Plus, shifting the responsibility of accepting new requests away from the IT department will likely be seen as a huge win for executive leadership and those that need to buy into the new request management process, as it will help to increase their influence in application management.

Just like anything else, a successful request management process starts with an end-to-end plan. The plan should address who is able to make requests, how requests are initiated, who receives the request, and how requests are categorized.

One of the initial decisions that needs to be made in the request management process is who has the authority to submit a change to begin with. There are basically three options, and each has benefits and consequences to consider. Ultimately, there is no best option, and the decision of how to proceed should attempt to maximize requests without overburdening the portfolio office with superfluous ideas.

The first option is to simply open the request form and allow anyone and everyone to submit new ideas for applications. The concept may not be as terrible as it sounds. Consider other forms of feedback in your organization where everyone is invited to participate, such as surveys or suggestion boxes. It would be extremely rare to see a suggestion box overflowing with ideas, and you can likely expect the same for project and application requests. Additionally, by opening the request process to everyone, no one can feel that they did not have an opportunity to be heard, and there is no excuse for someone to circumvent the process due to not being included. At the same time, we must abide by the core principles identified earlier and ensure that every request is treated equally, no matter how much of an oddball request it may seem to be. If you have a particularly large vocal organization and a comparatively small portfolio office, it's possible that you will start to lose sight of the forest for the trees, spending more time processing and analyzing inbound requests than actually working to accomplish them.

The second option is to only allow requests if they have been vetted by a team lead, manager, or supervisor. Or, only those in a managerial role can submit requests. This option keeps the field wide open, with the caveat that there needs to be some internal discussion ahead of time. It also avoids the awkward possibility of a request, making it through the process before the requestor's supervisor is even aware of the need. Ensuring some level of internal vetting may also increase buy-in from departmental stakeholders without sacrificing the openness and accessibility of the process itself.

The final option is to only allow designated individuals to submit requests. This scenario would work best for particularly large spread-out organizations, such as multisite hospitals. It may not only stifle some requests but also ensures that a certain amount of vetting has been done before a request reaches a final governance board. Keep in mind that designating individuals as having the authority to submit requests may be challenging, as well. After all, you are identifying someone who would have the ability to speak on behalf of a large number of people, and that person would have the ability to reject ideas before they are ever submitted before a governance committee, thereby inviting politics and favoritism to control the process, as opposed to a fair and balanced approach.

Once you have determined who is able to initiate requests, you will need to control how the requests get submitted, and there are a few options for this, as well. Some of the more common methods include committee-based requests, paper-based requests, and electronic form-based requests.

Committee-based requests involve the designation of a team or group that would evaluate requests prior to submission to the organization's official request management team. Although this may seem like more red tape and more committees to review the same request, this strategy would work well for large departments or those that are spread out across different areas of the organization. It ensures that there is consensus from the requesting department or team, and if you have chosen to designate specific people to submit the final request, it provides those person(s) with appropriate assurance that the request has been well-vetted, at least from within the given department. Additionally, this strategy allows for more thought-out and comprehensive requests that have more detailed requirements that are properly aligned to the organization's mission, thereby giving a higher probability that the request will eventually be approved and implemented. However, as you might expect, the overall process is more time consuming and may limit some individual's desire to submit new requests. They may find it easier to implement their own IT solutions in the shadows than risk putting in weeks or months of effort to justify their need, just to see if die before it even reaches the organization's governance board(s).

Paper-based requests, while seemingly antiquated, provide the easiest and most accessible method of proposing new project ideas. Paper-based requests do not necessarily mean hardcopy printouts and handwritten notes, but rather it can be a form in a standard word-processing program that can be quickly disseminated to interested parties. There is no committee to review the request, nor logins to memorize – just a standard form that is easy to create, modify, and distribute. Having a paper trail can also provide assurances regarding who is making and receiving the requests and when. However, working with paper-based forms can lead to poor version control, especially regarding the layout of the form. If you wish to make changes to the information being collected, it will be essential that you have a clear channel to communicate those changes, or you will risk having outdated forms completed for months and even years into the future. Forms can also be manipulated or completed in limited levels of detail, requiring more follow-up and analysis than should be needed. Additionally, relying on an inbox or email could result in "lost" requests, especially if there are breaks in the process or someone "forgets" to process one of the inbound requests. Therefore, it is critical that the process to manage inbound requests is not reliant on a single person and has a strong tracking mechanism in place.

Finally, requests could be made through an electronic form or application. This may be the most costly and complex to implement, but a tool that is well thought out can have a clear logical flow with required/optional fields and the ability to control who has the authority to submit requests. You may even be able to have different types of requests categorized in the system, such as those that may be initiated through individuals as ideas or suggestions versus those that have gone through a more detailed committee. If organizational requirements change, modifications to the form can be made quickly and in real time without having to worry about version control of the form itself. Additionally, electronic tools can include more features over time, including the ability for requestors to track their submissions through review and approval. However, just like any other electronic IT system, appropriate safeguards will need to be put into place to reduce or eliminate data corruption, lost requests, and other vulnerabilities. A system will also require an administrator to control security and access, as well as limit any potential downtime, so the tool can be readily and routinely available for new submissions.

Regardless of who can submit requests or how they get into the request management process, the most important guidelines to follow is to implement a process that is simple, fair, and accessible. This includes the types of questions that are asked in the initial request form. As you start to consider what information you want to collect, it's important to limit the information being requested upfront. It's quite possible that most of the information you really need, such as the impact on IT resources, server requirements, security implications, architecture, and other details, may not be known by your requestor or you may obtain incomplete or inaccurate information. Additionally, requiring significant technical details upfront may cause business areas of the organization to derive their own IT requirements, which may not be appropriate. Instead, it's more important to focus on the business need and what needs to be accomplished, and from there, the IT department can determine how to make that happen. Therefore, create a request intake form that only focuses on three areas that are of interest to everyone:

1. **What is being requested?** This could include a high-level scope statement and major project objectives. At this point, there is not a need to focus on specific details or requirements.
2. **Why is the project needed?** The justification for the project should include specific examples of how the request relates to the mission of the organization or what mandates are being met. It is acceptable to include information about when the project is needed, especially if it is to meet regulatory requirements, but it's important to note that

the requested timeline is just that: a request. An estimated timeline should never be promised until the request is approved, prioritized, and aligned with available IT and business resources.

3. **How much does it cost?** This may include both human and physical resources and whether funds have been allocated for the work. There should be a certain amount of caution with this question, as well. Often, detailed pricing from external vendors may not be available until procurement has started and requirements are defined, but you do not want the requestor conducting those activities until the project is approved and IT resources are available. Therefore, this should be limited to a high-level estimate based on research of similar applications and implementations. Alternately, this question may only focus on funding sources, or it could be eliminated entirely.

The sample project request form as shown in Figure 3.1 contains some of the minimal request details that you may want to collect from those that are making the initial submission.

One of the final steps in the initial submission process is to determine where the requests will be submitted. As noted earlier, it is strongly recommended that the IT department is not responsible for the collection of these requests. The project and portfolio office may eventually be responsible for the tracking, implementation, and final disposition of an application, but inbound requests should not go directly to that office. It is critical to ensure that every request is handled fairly in the same manner. Inserting the IT department into the acceptance of new requests could be perceived as adding influence or bias into that process. Therefore, inbound requests should be directed to a representative of the organization's project governance committee. Once received, the IT department could have a role in helping to elicit more detailed requirements, but ensuring that requests are submitted through a business (non-IT) process helps ensure impartiality.

After the request has been submitted, there should be some level of analysis, categorization, and handoff built into your request management plan. The initial request was internally slimmed down to the core objectives and business need for the project, but it does not provide enough detail for the governance committee to decide how the request should be prioritized, nor does it provide the IT department with enough information to determine the impacted human and physical resources. The process of analysis and categorization provides the detail to fill the gap between request and governance review.

[Organization Name]

New IT Project Request Form

[Project Name]

Please complete the following form to request all new IT projects, including new application installations, upgrades to existing applications, and major configuration modifications. Please note that the start date of this request is subject to governance approval, prioritization, and availability of appropriate IT resources. Please submit the completed form to the IT Governance Committee (ITGC).

General Information

Requestor Name:	Department:
Phone:	Email:
Has this request been reviewed by your department leadership? ◯ Yes ◯ No	
Requested Start: *mm/yyyy*	Estimated Duration: *XX months*

Request Information

Brief Description of Project
    [Describe the major objectives of the project, including what you are expecting to accomplish, any new applications or software that may be needed, any integrations with existing software, and any impacts or relationships to existing projects or applications].

Justification
Why is this project needed?
    [Describe how the project relates to the mission of the department or organization, and any potential return on investment that is expected with a successful implementation.]

Is this related to patient safety? ◯ Yes ◯ No

Is this related to a regulation or other mandate? ◯ Yes ◯ No

Funding Information
Estimated cost (initial):

Estimated cost (ongoing/maintenance):

Is funding available? ◯ Yes ◯ No

For Internal Use Only

Request Number:	Date Received:
ITGC Review Required?	Request Category:

IT Project Request Form v. 1.0 – Last Revised February 6, 2020

Figure 3.1 IT Project Request Form Template.

Once the request is received by the representative(s) of the governance committee, it should be shared with the project and portfolio office, who can assign a system or business analyst to the request to gather additional detail. Optimally, the analyst should be aware of the technical abilities of the organization, the overall architecture of existing IT systems, security and privacy mandates, and the ability to elicit both business and technical requirements from customers that may have limited-to-no IT experience. This is a tall order for most staff, which is why this role is so important, and given the number of requests that may need to be reviewed, it may even be a full-time position or broken up between multiple analysts with varying skill sets.

In organizations that do not have a dedicated analyst role, the work to define the project request may be handled by the representative of the governance committee, the lead of the project and portfolio office, or even a project manager, who is already familiar with working between business leads, technical stakeholders, and vendors. Some of the key initial questions that should be asked on any new project request include

1. **Do you already have a solution in mind?** In many cases, the requestor already knows what software they want to implement. Perhaps they saw a solution at a trade show, or they found a piece of software online that does exactly what they need. Even if a specific solution is anticipated, many organizations have procurement rules in place that require multiple bids against stated requirements, and government-based agencies may even have restrictions on the types of businesses that can work with them. In addition, there may be security and privacy regulations that would prevent the acquisition of specific solutions. Unless there is absolute certainty that a specific product can be purchased without restrictions, the focus should be on the business-driven requirements. Specific applications could be used to help identify requirements for the final solution, but naming the product this early in the process should be avoided.

2. **Does this involve an existing system?** This question may at first seem like a quick yes/no answer, followed by the name of the impacted system(s). For example, if the request is to upgrade a system in the Information Management Department, that system is clearly the system that is involved. However, the acquisition of brand-new applications may still involve existing systems, and questions like this are meant to drive in more detail. It is important to understand that it is rare for a request to have no impact on existing systems, unless it is a stand-alone

application that resides on an isolated server or workstation. In the healthcare industry especially, many vendors market their applications as being able to integrate with other systems. For example, the procurement of a new freezer could include a temperature monitoring system that needs to interface with a hospital-wide monitoring system. Or, a new laboratory instrument may need to pull patient data from the EHR or send results back to a lab information system. Careful consideration of the answer to this question must be made, and if there is any potential impact with another system, it's critical to understand what those impacts will be and if they are even technically feasible.

3. **Who or what is impacted? Or, who or what will benefit?** In addition to reviewing the technical impacts of existing systems, there are business functions to consider, as well. Regardless of the marketing used by vendors, many software applications will cause a disruption to existing processes, especially on business workflows. After all, the purpose of obtaining an upgrade or new application is usually to provide some benefit, such as speeding up or even automating existing processes. Changes to workflows will be disruptive, regardless of how much effort is made to maintain existing processes. Therefore, every project request should carefully consider the processes and procedures that are currently in place and determine how those will change. Also, consider the downstream impacts and risks that may not be obvious. For example, if you are going to implement a new web-based patient portal, will you have enough staff available to answer questions from patients on how to use it? If you are going to streamline the delivery of medications to inpatients, will your nurses and pharmacy staff be able to keep up with the demand? Continuing to ask deep-diving questions based on responses received to this initial one is key to understanding the overall impact of the project request.

4. **What are the business/functional requirements?** This question should be the main driver for what will be accomplished during the project. The more detail that can be elicited here will make the evaluation, procurement, and project management that much easier. While there is not a need to specify every detailed requirement at this point, there should be enough detail to fully describe what the requestor is trying to accomplish. It's important to note that some requestors may be excited to share countless requirements for the initial deployment of a new system as they try to make it be everything to everyone. However, it's possible that some of these requirements may not be technically feasible to implement or may take a considerable amount of time or money to complete.

In these situations, the analyst should work closely with the requestor to help separate mandatory requirements from those that would be "nice to have" but could certainly wait until a future project or implementation timeline. Another consideration in the collection of requirements is the driver behind the request. It is very easy to be swayed by the vast array of marketing materials, whitepapers, trade shows, vendor promotions, and demonstrations for healthcare solutions, and the requestor may find themselves more driven by the *product* as opposed to the expected *outcome*. If the requestor cannot explicitly identify the problem they are trying to solve, it's possible that the requested solution may not be in the best interest of the organization. Let the requestor define the problem, and allow the IT department to help identify a solution.

5. **What are the technical requirements?** It may be challenging to determine all the IT requirements at this stage, but some of the business needs may drive the technical objectives. For example, if the request is for an application that can be accessed from anywhere, there may be technical requirements for web-based solutions and dual-factor authentication for remote access. Or, there may be a need to procure additional hardware or workstations to increase accessibility on patient units. Additionally, there may be specific architectural or security requirements that place limits on how systems are implemented, which may ultimately drive the final product that is selected. Just as was done for the business-side requirements, there is no need to go into significant detail regarding these requirements, but there should be enough information here for decision makers to fully understand the impacts.

6. **What is the impact of not completing the request?** The original request form should have included some level of justification as to why the project is important and how it will benefit the department or organization. However, just as important to understand is the impact of not completing the request or even delaying it. This should not only be an easy question to answer for justifiable requests, but it also helps drive home the true business need and will help determine the priority of the request. There is a difference between solutions that fix problems that are "not optimal" versus those that pose an immediate and definite patient safety impact. Is the request driven on financial data, safety conditions, process improvement, or something else?

7. **When is this needed?** Just as there was a caution flag thrown in the initial request form, there needs to be caution when asking this question, as well. Most requestors will be honest and provide a reasonable

timeframe for when they expect work to start. However, requests that involve safety, security, and other mission-critical criteria may have timeframes of being needed "yesterday." It is not the responsibility of the analyst to determine whether the requested timeframe is reasonable, but there should at least be a question as to what is driving the timeframe. From there, the organization's governance and leadership can make a final judgment on the priority of the request. After all, there will only be so many resources available to complete the work, and if work exceeds capacity, tough decisions will need to be made on what work needs to stop to accommodate the new request(s).

After the request has been fully analyzed, it can be categorized and documented into a template that will make it easier for decision makers to understand what is needed. The first step is to determine whether the request requires a significant amount of work and multiple resources, and therefore would benefit from having a project manager coordinate the effort. Alternately, the request may be simple enough where the development of a project scope, workplan, and other artifacts would be unnecessary and may even take more time than the completion of the work to fulfill the request. Simple and routine changes should be managed via a change control process as part of the organization's overall operations and maintenance plans, which is discussed in more detail in Chapter 7. Defining the difference between day-to-day operations and new projects is not always a fixed line and is usually based on resource capacity and the level of control desired from leadership. A common method for drawing a distinction between the two is to set a workload threshold, or total hours to complete the request, after analysis is complete. For example, a task that requires <40 hours of work does not need to be managed as a project. Additional criteria can also be used, such as number of teams impacted, the level of visibility of the request, the impact of the change, or even whether the request is originating from a very important person in the organization. Regardless of how it's defined, the distinction needs to be clear, and someone (or a group) must be responsible for designating the initial category of the request.

If the request is determined to be a project, it will likely require more rigorous reviews from additional committees, including any project governance in the organization. To some stakeholders, this process may seem more cumbersome and filled with dreaded "red tape," so it's important to emphasize the importance of these reviews in the context of meeting mission objectives and prioritizing IT workload. To help make this process more meaningful, the data gathered by the system/business analyst should be captured in a standard format or document. When the requirements are known, but the end solution is not, the best document to create at this point is a business case.

A *business case* is focused on the justification for the change, as this will be the primary document used by governance committees and review boards to make approval and prioritization decisions. Although there is no global standard for what should be included in a business case, templates that provide the most benefit to the reader include

- **A definition of the problem:** What issue is trying to be solved by this project? It could be as simple as upgrading to the latest version of an application, as security vulnerabilities or lack of vendor support may be a risk with the current version. Or, it may be more complicated with various symptoms and causes.

- **The proposed solution to fix the problem:** This part of the business case should include the high-level business requirements that were identified during analysis, as well as the justification, funding, and return on investment provided by the original requestor. Just as important as the proposed solution are alternatives. Whether the customer likes it or not, there is rarely a single solution to fix a given problem, and there may be short- and long-term approaches that have varying levels of cost, resources, and time to implement. Providing alternatives gives more credence to the original request, as it demonstrates that serious methods have been considered to solve the initial problem, and the request is not simply borne out of a good marketing campaign from a vendor.

- **The risks and impacts:** Every new request will introduce some level of risk. After all, the request is to change some aspect of something, which in turn will have some level of impact on resources, operations, procedures, workflows, or even the external community. In order to fully understand the impacts of the request, both positive and negative, the risks and impacts should be clearly documented, along with their likelihood and mitigation strategies, as appropriate.

- **The stakeholders:** If this request were to be implemented, who would need to be included in those discussions? It may expand beyond just the IT and clinical staff and could include patients, marketing, or other organizations entirely. Providing an initial list of potential stakeholders will help define the scope of work, and it may even generate discussions about why certain groups are included or excluded. Those discussions are much more beneficial to occur at this stage of the project, rather than weeks or days before the activation.

Some examples of project requests that would necessitate the development of a business case could include

- A new application to track staff productivity and scheduling
- A document management system to store personnel files
- Replacing an existing nursing application with a new one
- Overhauling the hospital's paging system to including mobile devices and kiosks

Optimally, these requests are based on business needs and objectives, rather than a specific solution. However, there will be scenarios where both the requirements and the final solution are already known. In those cases, a business case may not be as beneficial, as there may not be alternatives available or the solution could be defined by a mandate or regulatory requirement. Some example of these requests could include

- Upgrade of operating system components due to security vulnerabilities
- Replacement of server-side hardware to adhere to new vendor specifications
- Integrating an existing software app with another existing software app
- Implementation of a new feature to comply with a national standard/ mandate

In cases where the solution is already known, it may be beneficial to start work on the project charter, which can be handed off to the project manager, should the project be approved. As noted in the previous chapter, the project charter is typically developed during project initiation, but if the major components of a charter are already known, they can be drafted now and then finalized once a project manager is assigned. Some of the information that could be included in a project charter at this stage include

- **The request:** This includes the description, high-level objectives, and overall justification for the project, as defined in the original request.
- **The deliverables:** Since the solution is already known, some of the technical requirements can be added, as well as the expected

milestones and timeline for the work. Information on budgets and funding may also be detailed enough to include in the charter.

- **The environment:** This includes an initial list of risks, assumptions, and constraints that could impact the project.
- **The involvement:** Just like the business case, the initial list of expected personnel that would be involved with the project can be included, as well as their roles and responsibilities. The internal and external stakeholders can also be defined here.

Once the project details have been captured and documented, the final step in the request process is handoff. Ultimately, every new project request should be considered for presentation at the organization's governance committee. However, there may be a need for additional internal reviews to ensure all relevant details are included. These reviews could include

- **Evaluation by the security and privacy team(s):** Due to the increasing levels of threats against healthcare systems, it is critical that new requests are reviewed by experts in the security and privacy office(s). There may be organizational standards that prohibit certain data to be hosted in cloud-based systems, or there may be a need to include encryption and other protective measures on data at rest and in transit. These requirements could have a dramatic effect in the overall timeline and workload of the project, so it's important that this work is known upfront, before any work begins.
- **Review by procurement officials:** It does not matter what a vendor tells you or how convincing they are, you will need to abide by the standards and practices set forth in your organization's procurement office. It's possible that small healthcare practices could procure the solutions they need off-the-shelf without much fanfare, but there is an increasing number of organizations that are writing rules and regulations when it comes to procurement, especially those in the government sectors, which may have legal consequences for improper acquisitions.
- **Review by technical architecture experts:** The increasing dependency on IT solutions commands more attention on the overall technical architecture that is in place within organizations. A formal architecture committee can help set standards for the implementation of new IT solutions, particularly when it comes to hardware and network configuration, as well as system integration, database standards, and required agent installations for application logging and operational review. The

proposed request may not initially be in alignment with these standards, so the inclusion of this group at this stage helps ensure that objectives and technical requirements are in alignment with defined standards.

Finally, all request documentation can be considered ready for final review. As you may have noticed, a request requires considerable analysis and input before review or approval, and the lack of these steps can lead to incomplete or misunderstood requirements. In turn, this leads to scope creep, change requests, and even more dreadful: failed projects. Developing a robust request management plan is not about creating more red tape, but it's more about ensuring that all potential projects are fully evaluated for their impact on the organization before any final decisions are made. This is the most fair and transparent process that can be implemented to ensure success and satisfied customers.

Before we can begin the initial implementation project, there is one more review that should take place, and that occurs through the organization's governance committee. The next chapter will explore what governance includes, why it is necessary, and how to implement a successful governance process in your organization.

Chapter 4

Governance

We should not prioritize on the basis of project profitability, but
rather on how this profitability is affected by delay.

– Donald G. Reinertsen
*The Principles of Product Development Flow:
Second Generation Lean Product Development*

Project and portfolio **governance** refers to the framework that an organization may establish to make decisions on the relevancy and priority of new
project requests. Having a robust governance process in place ensures that
the right projects are done at the right time, while ensuring alignment to
the organization's mission and vision. Projects can be major undertakings,
requiring multiple resources, time, and money, so it is crucial that these
efforts are understood and monitored on a regular basis. This chapter will
provide a guide on developing a governance board, while reviewing its
membership, responsibilities, and deliverables that are produced to ensure
its success.

Consider the current role of information technology (IT) in your organization as it relates to approving and prioritizing IT projects. Is your IT
department responsible for establishing a roadmap for IT projects, and if
so, is that appropriate? Certainly, the IT department has a major voice in the
implementation of IT projects, as they should be setting standards for architecture, management, security, privacy, disaster recovery, and everything else
associated with ensuring that applications are readily available and supported. However, shouldn't every application in an organization's portfolio
somehow drive or support the business practices? And if so, why does the

business not have a stronger role in reviewing these IT projects? In some cases, it may be a feeling that it's "outside of your scope of work." If you are in charge of a nursing department, for example, you are going to be more concerned that your nurses have the skills and training needed to take care of patients and may wish to leave all the IT "stuff" to those who know more about technology. You may identify technical solutions to help your staff accomplish their roles, but you would rather have the vendor or IT take care of all the details to implement it. However, the nursing department is only one component of a larger healthcare business, and the IT department will be receiving requests from multiple departments, stakeholders, and external entities. As the lead of an IT department, you may think that certain projects have a higher priority than others, or you may wish to carve the easiest path forward by completing "easy" projects first, or by allowing politics to drive workload by accommodating the more important stakeholders in the organization, or working on projects that have the highest visibility or likelihood to succeed.

Having an organization where responsibilities are siloed into distinct roles of technology vs. business can create disagreements on the priority of IT projects. Most of the projects that are undertaken in a healthcare organization likely have some impact to patient safety or satisfaction, whether it's decreasing the likelihood of certain occurrences, or increasing checkpoints in a critical workflow process. Few would argue that projects dealing with safety are not important, but when the number of project requests exceeds the capacity of staff to do the work, there needs to be some determination of priority. If the IT department makes that decision, it would seem as though the tail is wagging the dog, so to speak, and there would be questions about why IT is making decisions that impact clinical staff. On the business end, the requestor will certainly champion their own project request over others, so if the decision is escalated to executive leadership (the C-suite), will executive leadership have the information they need to make the best decision for the organization? The key is to develop a process for IT projects where everyone can feel represented, and likewise, everyone becomes accountable for that work.

There are additional signs that you may experience that will constitute the need for project governance, including

- **Failed IT initiatives:** Projects fail, and in some cases, for very preventable reasons. Often, failures are cited due to inadequate project planning or lack of requirements or poor documentation or inexperienced project managers. However, a common theme, even with these causes, typically comes back to communication failures. Ensuring that projects are appropriately monitored and communicated amongst multiple stakeholders helps keep everyone accountable to each other.

■ **Unintended project impacts on the organization:** If the right stakeholders are not included in the project from the beginning, it's possible that there will be impacts and consequences that were never considered. It's impossible for any one project manager or team member to understand every dynamic and possible risk for a project, so bringing together a community will only help to ensure that more stakeholders, risks, and impacts are identified early.

■ **Limited organizational oversight of IT projects:** If you are not being held accountable for specific processes, or even specific projects, it's more likely that they will start to fall astray, especially if there is not a strong driver to getting the project done, or there are competing priorities that seem more interesting or important. Having a shared accountability is the key to successfully complete all relevant projects, or having an agreed-upon approach to eliminate or deprioritize projects that show little value. This is particularly important if the organization's priorities change, which could lead to the removal of certain applications altogether.

A project and portfolio governance management strategy will provide the appropriate accountability, direction, and oversight for all IT projects. In order to ensure it is successful, there are a few components that should be in place ahead of time. First, just like the request management process, you must have buy-in from executive-level decision makers. It may be helpful to draft a plan of how governance will interact with the C-suite and what its role will be in the organization. Keep in mind that the C-suite has ultimate responsibility to determine the direction of the organization. Therefore, the governance committee should be a recommending body that serves to provide information, justification, and advice to executive management. This helps to reaffirm the accountability of IT projects throughout the organization.

Second, the organization should already have formal processes in place for project management, which should include standard operating procedures, methodologies, and templates for project documentation. Once a project is approved, the governance committee will likely want to track its status, and if you do not have a means of controlling projects, the entire process is likely to fail. Some of the basics of good project management principles were discussed in Chapter 2, and you must be able to prove that those processes are active and in place.

Third, careful consideration should be made as to who will represent project requests at the governance committee. The group should be comprised of a diverse array of interested and engaged stakeholders to represent all aspects of the organization, including section leads, steering and medical committees, purchasing and contracting leads, prescribers, and electronic health record (EHR) end users. These members would be given voting rights for all projects that need review or prioritization. The IT department should have a voice in the meetings and should provide subject matter expertise, but just like the request process, it would not be appropriate for IT to vote on which projects should take priority over others. By setting up the governance committee in this way, there is greater pressure on the organization to provide accountability for IT projects. Other nonvoting members could include any deputies appointed by the C-suite, as well as someone who is well versed in budgetary aspects of the organizations, such as the Chief Financial Officer (CFO). Occasionally a request may be submitted with a strong justification but may lack the necessary funding to accomplish the requirements. In that case, the CFO can help with reviewing financial options or even petition the C-suite on behalf of the requestor for the funds to accomplish the project based on the priority determined by the governance committee. This shared responsibility is shown in Figure 4.1.

One of the central figures that is not illustrated in the diagram is the chair of the governance board. He or she should not be a voting member, but they must serve as a champion of the process, ensuring that all stakeholders are well versed in the requirements for new project reviews, and holding people accountable when projects are implemented without going through the proper channels. Accountability could include suspension of a representative from a membership role in the committee or even the removal of an unapproved application. These actions must be taken to ensure compliance with stated practices and must also be upheld by the highest levels of the organization, hence the importance of buy-in. The role of the chair should not be given to a member of the IT department, nor should it include membership from the C-suite. Instead, the chair would optimally be a representative from one of the groups defined earlier, preferably with great clinical expertise to help demonstrate that he or she has a fair understanding of medical practices and requirements.

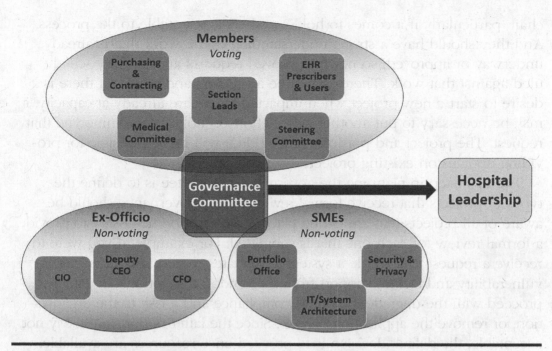

Figure 4.1   Governance environment.

After the membership is defined, you can begin to document a charter for the governance board to officially designate their role in the approval and prioritization of project requests. The charter should include

- The **name** of the committee (for the sake of this exercise, we will call the group the "IT Governance Committee" or ITGC).
- The **effective date** or duration of the committee, or the time between review of the charter and committee membership, including the chair.
- The **purpose** of the committee.
- The **delegation of authority**, being careful to indicate that the committee is limited to making recommendations.
- The **deliverables** that will be created as a result of this committee.
- A list of each voting member, the committee chair, any Subject Matter Experts (SMEs), and their **roles and responsibilities**.

The roles and responsibilities of the voting members should routinely be stressed upon the committee, so everyone is aware of their influence on the direction of the organization. They must be prepared to defend the mission and vision of the organization by ensuring all projects are justifiably related to its strategic plan. They should be ready to defend decisions made by the chair, particularly if it comes to holding others accountable to the process. And they should have a strong understanding of the work that is already underway or approved, so newly approved requests are properly scheduled against that work. There should be an understanding that if there is a desire to start a new project when impacted teams are already at capacity, it may be necessary to put another active effort on hold to accommodate that request. The project and portfolio office (PPO) will be responsible for providing updates on existing projects.

The next step in planning the governance committee is to define the types of projects that receive formal review. While governance should be aware of all projects that are taking place, it may not be necessary to provide a formal review for each one that is submitted. For example, if you were to receive a request to upgrade a system to the latest version due to security vulnerability and lack of support from the vendor, the options are either to proceed with the upgrade, be out of compliance and a risk to the organization, or remove the application entirely. Since the latter options are likely not acceptable, the default decision is to proceed once resources are available. However, as project requests become more complex, expensive, or unique, it may be necessary for governance to provide recommendations on whether they should be approved. The image below provides some examples of the types of projects that could be submitted and an example of where a committee may elect to intervene. Of course, there is no global standard for what requires formal review, so that line will depend on the organization's priorities, frequency of committee meetings, the number of projects expected for review at any given time, as well as funding and resource constraints. The definition of what gets reviewed should be considered a guideline and would not be part of the charter for the committee (Figure 4.2).

The type and quantity of requests that are reviewed by the governance committee will depend on the frequency of meetings. The regularity of meetings should be carefully considered. The first point to consider is the role of the attendees in the organization. Most likely, you are including senior-level leads who have limited time allotted on their schedule, so meeting as frequently as weekly or monthly may not be feasible for them. Additionally, limiting the number of times the group convenes will also require requestors to be strategic and consider their needs well in advance. Conversely, limited meetings could increase the likelihood of staff circumventing the process to get their work accomplished sooner. To combat the frustrations of limited meeting schedules, you may wish to add emergency review procedures for projects that cannot wait until the next formal

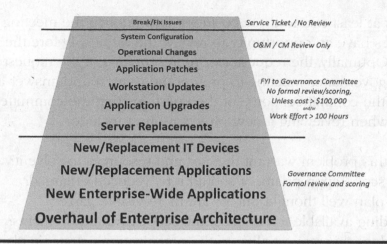

Figure 4.2   Request examples.

meeting. Emergency requests would need sufficient justification and should still undergo the same careful documentation and planning used in the request management process, but it allows projects to proceed on a faster timeframe while still utilizing the organization's governance process.

As with any meeting, a formal agenda helps to provide direction and organization to the committee. It is recommended that an individual is identified as the secretary for the governance meetings, who would be responsible for composing the agenda, gathering and distributing documentation, and taking detailed minutes. At a minimum, the following components should be included in every governance meeting agenda:

Announcements

This is a generic catch-all topic that allows attendees to provide updates on major activities that could impact project resources, funding, or timelines. This time can also be used to provide a review of the recommendations from the last meeting, and the final decision(s) made by hospital leadership.

Review of New Project Requests

This should be a review of all projects that met the appropriate criteria for review. The documentation provided to the committee should include the original IT project request, as well as the business case or project charter that was put together by the analyst. The goal should be to distribute these documents at least two to three business days prior to the meeting so that all attendees have an opportunity to review the request before the group convenes. Optimally, the requestor or representative of the request should attend the governance meeting to present the request and answer any questions from the committee. Some of the questions that the committee should be asking when reviewing a new project request include

- Does this problem warrant the cost and resources to solve it?
- Is the scope appropriate, or should it be reduced/enlarged?
- Is the plan well thought out, or are there visible gaps?
- Is funding available to complete the scope and requirements?
- How does this request align to the organization's strategic plan?
- Are there other applications already in-house that can solve this problem?
- How will you know when all objectives have been met?
- What are the impacts of delaying the start beyond the requested time?
- What are the expected deliverables, and when will they be ready?
- How should status reports be brought to the attention of the committee?
- Can this application be used to resolve other issues in the organization?
- What risks could contribute to the project's failure?
- What other stakeholders should be included?
- Who will be responsible for maintaining the application once it's live?

Once all requests have been thoroughly reviewed, the committee should make a final recommendation on the request, which could range from approval, approval with modifications, deferment until additional research is completed, or outright denial. It is highly recommended that no new approvals occur until there are resources available to complete the request. There are several methods that can be used to come to a consensus on this recommendation, including a vote during the meeting, or anonymous ballots collected after the meeting has concluded. However, this method employs a simplistic yes/no view of the projects, and it's unlikely that any projects will receive an overwhelming "no" vote, especially given the thought and consideration that went into the analysis of the request before it even came to the committee. Therefore, it's more important to evaluate the impact and value of the request, which in turn can drive a final priority score for the eventual project.

There are a wide variety of options to choose from when determining how to score and present project requests, some of which are described below. It's important to understand the culture of your organization, who will be involved in the scoring, and what knowledge they have of the subject matter when choosing the best approach. Choosing the appropriate method should be done carefully, to keep scores fair across all projects. If you decide to change approaches later, the prioritization that was given to earlier projects may no longer be applicable. Therefore, it's important to choose the best method for your group and remain as consistent as possible.

■ **Weighted Scoring:** Each project is provided several different criteria to help determine the impact (difficulty, funding, and work effort) and value (benefit, return on investment (ROI), and satisfaction).

Some examples of criteria to measure *impact* could include
  – Funding required for initial implementation
  – Funding required for ongoing maintenance
  – Timeline to complete work
  – Human resources required
  – IT complexity compared to existing systems
  – Level of integrations with other systems
  – Level of training required
  – Number of stakeholders impacted

Some examples of criteria to measure *value* could include
  – Impact to patient care/quality
  – Impact to patient/customer satisfaction
  – Alignment to organization's strategy
  – Areas to benefit from the request
  – Improvements to efficiencies of operations
  – Improvements to system reliability/quality
  – Financial return on investment
  – Impact to employee engagement

Each of these criteria should be scored based on clearly defined values. This helps to ensure that all voting members have the same understanding when scoring a project. An example of these defined values is shown in Table 4.1.

■ **PICK Chart:** Originally developed by Lockheed Martin to help categorize new ideas as part of a lean development program (often associated with Six Sigma), this simple chart can be used in the governance process to determine if a request is **P**ossible (easy, but low value), should be **I**mplemented (easy, with high value), **C**hallenging (hard, but high value), or should be **K**illed (hard, and low value). Based on the information gathered through the weighted scoring technique, requests can

Table 4.1 Sample of Defined Values for Selected Criteria

	Impact Analysis				Value Analysis			
	Initial Funding	Timeline	Resources	Training	Strategic Plan	Satisfaction	Reliability	Financial ROI
	Weight = 25%	Weight = 25%	Weight = 35%	Weight = 15%	Weight = 25%	Weight = 25%	Weight = 15%	Weight = 35%
	High = 5 ≥$100 K	**High = 5** ≥2 years	**High = 5** ≥10 staff	**High = 5** Full training	**High = 5** 90%–100% aligned	**High = 5** High satisfaction	**High = 3** Improvements	**High = 5** ≤3 years
	Medium = 3 $100–$1 K	**Medium = 3** 1–2 years	**Medium = 3** 5–10 staff	**Medium = 3** Refresher only	**Medium = 2** 50%–90% aligned	**Medium = 3** Low satisfaction	**Medium = 3** No change	**Medium = 3** 3–5 years
	Low = 1 <$1,000	**Low = 1** <1 year	**Low = 1** <5 staff	**Low = 1** No training	**Low = 0** <50% aligned	**Low = 0** No/neg. impact	**Low = 1** Unpredictable	**Low = 1** 5+ years/no ROI

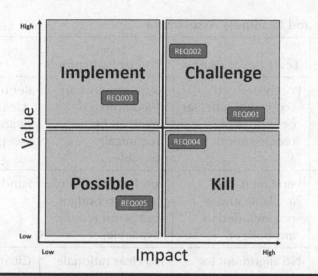

Figure 4.3   PICK chart.

be plotted on a PICK chart to provide a visual representation of the value and impact on an organization (Figure 4.3).

■ **Risk and Readiness Assessment:** You will find that every request carries some level of risk, and despite the request analysis that occurred prior to governance, there is a possibility that the project is not defined enough to be considered "ready" for implementation. Conducting a risk and readiness assessment can help determine if the request should be approved, or if modifications may be necessary prior to being given a green light (Table 4.2).

■ **Human Resource Assessment:** The one component in common with every IT request is that it will take some level of work from the hospital's IT department. Even when applications are hosted in the cloud and the vendor promises to do all of the heavy-lifting themselves, there will still need to be some involvement from the local IT group to ensure that connections are active and secure, architecture expectations are followed, privacy controls are in place, and support mechanisms have been developed. Projects that have strong justifications and support from the governance committee will still need to be prioritized amongst the other efforts underway by the IT department. Conducting an analysis of staffing requirements is a good way to plan early and schedule projects when resources are available. In turn, this also sets appropriate expectations as to when work can begin (Table 4.3).

Table 4.2   Risk and Readiness Assessment

	Level 1 (Not Ready)	Level 2 (Needs Evaluation)	Level 3 (Ready)
Project scope	Poorly defined scope with unclear or impossible requirements.	Requirements are incomplete or may not be technically feasible.	Requirements are clear and attainable within the defined scope.
Funding	Funding is not available and is not included in any budget.	Funding has been added to budget but is not readily available.	Funding is available.
Project justification	No alignment to strategic plan, and alternatives seem to be more compelling to resolve issues.	No clear rationale why alternative solutions cannot be acceptable.	Clear and defined justification indicates this request is the only acceptable option to resolve issues.
Impact risk	High level of risk to implement.	Medium level of risk to implement.	Low or acceptable risk to implement.
IT/architecture	Deviates from IT standards and practices.	Requires limited modifications to standard IT architecture.	Clear alignment to existing architecture and standards.

Table 4.3   Human Resource Assessment

	Time Commitment, in Hours, by Quarter				
	FY2020, Q1	FY2020, Q2	FY2020, Q3	FY2020, Q4	FY2021, Q1
Project manager	75	50	50	50	60
Server admin	25	30	10	10	5
Network admin	10	25	5	5	5
App. build/config	10	20	65	80	40
Tester	5	10	25	75	25
Trainer	5	5	20	50	60
Vendor	50	50	50	50	50
Customer	25	25	25	35	40

Table 4.4 Project Prioritization Matrix

Request	Value Score			Impact Score			Resource Needs		Patient Safety?	Regulatory Mandate?	Priority
	Max	Min	Mean	Max	Min	Mean	Qty.	Time			
REQ001	4	2	3.1	5	3	4.6	21	9,474	No	Yes	3
REQ002	5	4	4.6	5	2	3.2	15	7,238	Yes	No	2
REQ003	5	2	3.4	3	2	2.4	7	2,365	Yes	No	1
REQ004	4	1	2.9	4	2	3.1	8	3,876	No	No	5
REQ005	3	1	2.1	3	1	2.7	5	1,200	No	No	4

Once the committee has completed a full evaluation of the request, there should be enough data available to prioritize the project amongst the others in the active workload. By evaluating not just the value of the project but also the impact to the organization and resources, it becomes clear that the projects that bring the most value may not necessarily be the ones that should have the highest priority, or you may risk utilizing too many resources at the same time. Conversely, picking out the low hanging fruit and finishing the easy projects first may not actually bring much benefit to the organization. Therefore, careful consideration should be made when evaluating the scores of each project and creating a ranking that is routinely fair and efficient. The matrix in Table 4.4 demonstrates how five unique requests could be ranked.

Note that there is no perfect equation that can automatically create these rankings, as there will always be other considerations that cannot be boiled down to a single number, such as resource availability, interest of the stakeholders in the C-suite, public and customer perception/satisfaction, relation to patient safety issues or regulatory requirements, and general intrinsic value of the project. However, this exercise will provide leadership and stakeholders with confidence that each request was carefully considered before a final recommendation was made. Ultimately, these rankings and recommendations will require a final decision from executive leadership of the organization.

Review of Existing Project Requests

After new projects have been reviewed, the governance committee should also take on a role of active monitoring of existing projects. This does not take away from the role of the PPO, which is ultimately accountable for all projects and applications within the organization's portfolio. The governance committee's role with existing projects includes

- **Evaluating Project Performance:** There are several ways to evaluate the performance of existing projects. For high-visibility or high-priority projects, the committee may ask the project manager or another stakeholder representative to provide a briefing on the project. That representative should be prepared to share the current status, including schedule, budget, scope, and active risks and issues. One common methodology that project managers can use to demonstrate project performance is through the process of Earned Value Management (EVM). EVM considers the work that has been completed to date, as well as the time and cost it has taken to do so. That information is then compared against the original project baseline to determine if the project is ahead or behind schedule or cost. Being called to provide a briefing should be a routine part of the governance process and should not be reserved exclusively to call poor-performing projects to task, although that would certainly be an appropriate place for that review to occur.

    Additionally, the representative from the PPO should always provide a dashboard of all active projects so that the committee can understand the current workload of the department. This information should be derived from a consolidation of work effort across all projects. Most professional project management tools can gather this information electronically, but if such a tool is not available, this data will need to be manually collected from each project manager (PM). More likely than not, there will always be a' higher demand than the capacity of the office can handle. This will always create some additional constraint across multiple projects, such as increased timelines, excessive costs, decreased quality, or employee overtime. Indicating an appropriate waterline for optimal project management capacity will help the committee to understand where those constraints lie. The project dashboard below provides one possible way to consolidate this information into a single view. In this case, projects are aligned to a Gantt chart, clearly showing where projects are in the timeline (Figure 4.4).

- **Reviewing Resource Allocation:** A waterline on a project Gantt chart provides a general estimate as to resource capacity. However, every project is unique, and a waterline does little to show where overallocation may be occurring. Therefore, the PPO should develop a resource allocation matrix for review, showing a consolidated view of work hours across all active

Project	Value	Impact	Status	Timeline							
				FY20-Q1	FY20-Q2	FY20-Q3	FY20-Q4	FY21-Q1	FY21-Q2	FY21-Q3	
EHR upgrade	3.1	4.2	On Track	Plan	Plan	Exec.	Exec.	Exec.	Exec.	Go-Live	
Data center migration ⚷	2.5	4.1	Delayed	Plan	Exec.	Migrate	Migrate	Migrate	Close		
Lab system replacement	3.5	3.0	On Track	Exec.	Exec.	Exec.	Exec.	Go-Live	Close		
Clinical document rebuild ☣	4.2	2.2	On Track	Exec.	Exec.	Exec.	Go-Live	Close			
Genetic pedigree ☣	4.5	3.1	Delayed	On Hold	Exec.	Exec.	Go-Live	Close			
Telehealth portal ☣	4.8	3.9	On Track	Exec.	Exec.	Go-Live	Close				
Phone replacement ⚷	1.5	3.7	On Track	Exec.	Go-Live	Close					
Project Waterline: Optimal Project Management Capacity is 7 Active Projects											
Clinical device upgrade ⚷	1.4	1.6	On Track	Upgrade	Upgrade	Close					
Workstation Replacement	2.8	2.1	Delayed	Upgrade	Close						

☣ = Patient Safety Project

⚷ = Regulatory/Mandated Project

Figure 4.4 Project Dashboard.

projects. To create this matrix, there first needs to be an understanding of how much time each team or individual has allocated for the project work. In most cases, a given resource or team will not be 100% dedicated to any one project, nor is it likely that someone's job is dedicated solely to the implementation of new projects. Rather, resources typically need to divide their time across administrative functions, such as timecard reporting, training, supervision, and trouble ticket resolution, as well as operational functions, such as developing small change requests as part of an organization's configuration management program. Therefore, it may be necessary to evaluate historical timesheets submitted by employees to determine how much time they can allocate to new project activities. In the absence of detailed timesheets, this information can be gathered through surveys and discussions with team leads and front-line supervisors and managers. It's probable that some teams may only be able to dedicate 10%–20% of the working week to new projects, which would equate to only 4–8 hours per person. Even project managers cannot grant 100% of their time to projects due to other general administrative duties.

Once you have determined the number of available hours for a given team or individual, you can compare that to the total number of work hours allocated to those person(s) based on all active projects. This will provide a good overview of which teams are at/near/overcapacity and may suffer from taking on additional project work. This information can be documented and highlighted on the matrix, as shown in Table 4.5.

Table 4.5 Resource Allocation

	Available Hours	January	% Allocation	February	% Allocation	March	% Allocation
Project managers	320	350	109	330	103	300	94
Server admins	150	155	103	105	70	85	57
Network admins	75	75	100	70	93	60	80
App. build/ configs	210	180	86	220	105	150	71
Testers	125	120	96	110	88	95	76
Trainers	100	110	110	70	70	40	40

While this provides a quick overview, there are a few caveats that the governance committee should understand when evaluating this chart. First, if a team is overallocated, that does not necessarily mean that they are working overtime. It could simply mean that they have less time in the day to complete their operational duties, which in turn could put the organization at risk. Likewise, a team that is underallocated does not mean they have a lack of work on their plate. It's possible that these teams are working on outstanding technical issues that are not associated with projects, or the number of available hours may need to be updated. Another important consideration is that this chart only reflects work that is planned and/or underway. Projects that have not started or are still in their early planning phases may not have the details necessary to understand the actual workload requirements, so as the timeline stretches further into the future, more projects will be completed, and the overall allocation will decrease. However, in that same time, more projects will start, and those hours will increase, even though it's not shown in the matrix.

- **Reviewing Project Prioritization:** As new requests arrive, it's perfectly appropriate to evaluate the prioritization of past projects. Projects that have low value and unproportionally high complexity may routinely slide to the bottom of the list. You can expect that projects will always continue to arrive, and a backlog will always be present, so how will those projects ever start? One option is to add a date of when the project was requested to the list of pending projects. As a project request ages, that criteria could be used to increase its overall priority. Likewise, the committee may choose to completely remove old requests that provide little value to the organization.

- **Removing Obstacles:** Occasionally, a project will face unexpected challenges. These challenges could be in the form of funding sources, resource availability, vendor responsiveness, or even a lack of direction from project sponsors. It's primarily the PM's job to identify those challenges and find ways to avoid them. However, in rare situations where the PM has exhausted all possible means to keep the project moving forward, the project can be returned to the governance board for additional direction. Keep in mind that the committee is comprised of high-level managers and leads, so whenever possible, issues should be handled within the confines of the project.

- **Providing Feedback on Changes:** If a project scope and charter were approved through the governance framework, significant modifications may also need their blessing before they can proceed. In some cases, this may be due to a substantial change request or unexpected regulatory requirement. Every project should have a change management process built in, which describes how to document the change and its impacts so that it can be referred to the project sponsor for a decision. However, if the change is expected to change the resources required or the overall timeline, there's a good possibility that those changes will prevent new requests from even starting. It's important for the governance committee to know what major changes are being requested, and in turn, they can provide feedback and recommendations on how to proceed. In some cases, that may mean that a well-intentioned change request may need to be deferred to a separate project so that other higher-priority requests can proceed. Additionally, some project sponsors may elect to defer difficult decisions or those with wide-ranging impacts to the governance committee for approval.

■ **Placing Projects on Hold:** Occasionally, you may have a new request that is deemed to have a high priority for the organization, but the resources required to complete the work are already at or near capacity. This is where the human resource assessment described earlier can come into play. By using those estimates, along with the resource allocation matrix for active projects, it's possible that some active projects will need to temporarily stop or have their scopes reduced in order to accommodate the new request(s).

■ **Canceling Projects:** Although no one wants to admit to the failure of a project, there are times when expectations are not being met, and tough decisions need to be made to cancel an active project. Sometimes the cancelation could be due to external factors like changes in regulations. In other cases, a new project request has taken a higher priority or has rendered an old request to be obsolete. In any case, just as the committee has giveth, it can taketh away. Of course, even that would ultimately be a recommendation back to the C-suite for a final decision.

The decisions and recommendations from the governance committee meeting should be fully documented and presented to senior C-suite leadership within a week of the meeting. Typically, the presentation would be conducted by the chair of the governance committee. There should be written confirmation of the final decisions of the recommendations that were presented to the organization's leadership, and those decisions should be communicated back to the original requestor(s), either by the chair of the committee or by another designee, such as the lead of the PPO. Once the final decisions are made, the approved projects are turned over to the PPO to assign project managers and start the projects as soon as resources and schedules allow.

By implementing a governance framework into your organization, you can be assured of better management of inbound requests that are prioritized and scheduled in a fair and streamlined fashion. Some of the other outcomes that you can expect through a formal governance include

- Project scopes, objectives, and requirements that are clearly defined and reviewed by multiple parties.
- An improved understanding of project and portfolio processes from across the organization, where everyone becomes accountable to each other.
- Better alignment of new projects to the mission, vision, and strategic plans of the organization.
- The development of detailed project reports and metrics that can be comprehended by a wide swath of the organization (not just the PMs or the IT department).
- More engagement and involvement from project stakeholders, customers, and sponsors throughout the project lifecycle.
- Empowerment of appropriate project teams, project managers, and stakeholders at the right time.

Now that there is an understanding of how to set up a governance framework, let's evaluate how this would be put into practice. We will use a sample project request for a Bar Code Medication Administration (BCMA) system and will use that example throughout the remainder of this text to demonstrate how it would flow from request to governance to initial implementation, through operations/maintenance and finally to disposition. At this point, we will assume that the request was received through the appropriate channels, and analysis of the request has been completed as described in the prior chapter. Now, the original request and business case are ready to be presented to the governance committee. An example of the request and business case is shown in Figures 4.5 and 4.6.

After evaluating the request, the analyst and PPO have determined that this request meets the criteria to be presented to the full governance committee. Dr Josh Edwards (requestor) has agreed to present this project, and

General Information

Requestor Name: Dr Josh Edwards	**Department:** Nursing
Phone: 301-555-7863	**Email:** jedwards@myhospital.org
Has this request been reviewed by your department leadership? ● Yes ○ No	
Requested Start: *02/2021*	**Estimated Duration:** *20 months*

Request Information

Brief Description of Project

The purpose of this request is to implement a new Bar Code Medication Administration (BCMA) application throughout the hospital. This system will be integrated with the existing barcode technologies for Positive Patient Identification. This project will require new workflows to be developed and documented across multiple departments, including nursing, pharmacy, prescribers, respiratory therapy, and IT staff.

Justification

Why is this project needed?

The barcode-enabled, automated point-of-care technology solution is intended to address hospital-wide processes for medication administration. This relates directly to Good Hope Hospital's mission of patient safety, as it includes verification of the right patient, right drug, right dose, right strength, right time and right route of administration.

Is this related to patient safety? ● Yes ○ No

Is this related to a regulation or other mandate? ○ Yes ● No

Funding Information

Estimated cost (initial): $500,000 which includes the cost of equipment
Estimated cost (ongoing/maintenance): $25,000 per year for vendor support

Is funding available? ● Yes ○ No

Figure 4.5 BCMA project request.

the committee has provided the following feedback regarding the value, impact, and readiness (Tables 4.6 and 4.7).

The PPO worked with the system analyst to identify impacted resources and provided the following assessment of the impact on IT resources (Table 4.8).

Problem Definition

Current hospital procedures state that after a staff nurse has pulled a medication for administration, the nurse should manually verify the proper dose, strength and time against the electronic medical record contained in the hospital's EHR. The nurse must also verify the correct patient based on existing wristband practices. Finally, the nurse charts the medication as given in the EHR. While seemingly straightforward, the number of manual processes can lead to human error, and hospital records have shown several close calls in the past 12 months. On average, there have been 15 errors for every 5,000 medications administered. In one case, a patient was given the same medication twice because of a charting error, and in another a patient with the last name of "Testa" was almost given a dangerous dose of a research medication because the clinician thought she was a test/dummy patient. These errors could have resulted in severe patient reactions or even fatalities, which makes it essential to deploy a new application that can help reduce the likelihood of these occurrences. A Bar Code Medication Administration (BCMA) system will help confirm the five patient rights and serve as an assurance that a medication is administered at the correct time, dose and to the right patient.

Proposed Solution / Requirements

- Implement a new BCMA software tool.
- The BCMA shall be integrated with the existing EHR, allowing a single point of documentation.
- The BCMA shall use the existing barcode patient identification system and associated scanners.
- All medications shall have available barcodes.
- All impacted staff shall be notified and trained on any new workflows.
- The project will be considered successful and completed once all units are "up" with BCMA.

Risks and Impacts

Constraints

- Computers do not have the BCMA client installed.
- Lack of integration between the barcode patient identification system and the BCMA system.
- Current patient wristband barcodes unable to be scanned into BCMA.
- Weak wireless strength/unreliable connectivity.

Assumptions

- The new workflows are adopted by all stakeholders.
- The application configuration supports the approved workflows.
- A lesson learned meeting will be held after each unit is implemented in production to "learn" for the next unit being implemented.
- Two weeks is enough time between unit implementations, to complete all necessary work.

Figure 4.6 BCMA business case.

Table 4.6   Evaluation of BCMA: Initial Scores from Governance

Impact Analysis				Value Analysis			
Initial Funding	Timeline	Resources	Training	Strategic Plan	Satisfaction	Reliability	Financial ROI
High = 5 ≥$100 K	**Medium = 3** 1–2 years	**High = 5** ≥10 FTE	**High = 5** Full training	**High = 5** 90%–100% aligned	**High = 5** High satisfaction	**High = 3** Improvements	**Medium = 3** 3–5 years
Weighted average: 4.5				Weighted average: 4.0			

Table 4.7   Evaluation of BCMA: Risk and Readiness Assessment

	Risk and Readiness Level
Project scope	**Level 2 (needs evaluation)** Project scope is too large; recommend reducing to ten inpatient units to start
Funding	**Level 3 (ready)** Funding is available
Project justification	**Level 3 (ready)** Clear and defined justification
Impact risk	**Level 2 (needs evaluation)** There are multiple stakeholders with varying requirements that need to be confirmed
IT/architecture	**Level 3 (ready)** Aligns to existing architectural standards

One of the outcomes of the governance committee discussions was a consensus that while this project is clearly important, it requires a significant amount of work and commitment from many resources in the organization. Due to the risk of varying requirements and the potential impact on organizational workflows, the committee has recommended that the project scope be reduced to only include ten inpatient units in the initial implementation. If successful, a separate project should be requested to expand beyond the ten initial units.

This strategy and priority recommendation was presented to hospital leadership, who agreed and approved the scope with the stated modifications. This example project would now be ready for scheduling by the PPO. The next chapter will walk through the initial implementation of a new application.

Table 4.8   Evaluation of BCMA: Human Resource Assessment

	Time Commitment, in Hours, by Quarter					
	FY2020, Q4	*FY2021, Q1*	*FY2021, Q2*	*FY2021, Q3*	*FY2021, Q4*	*FY2022, Q1*
Project manager	400	300	300	300	300	400
Server admin	75	100	75	25	25	50
Network admin	50	150	50	20	20	40
App. build/config	25	250	450	450	450	475
Tester	25	50	100	100	150	100
Trainer	25	25	35	100	200	100
Vendor	300	300	300	300	300	300
Customer	75	75	75	75	100	125

Chapter 5

Initial Implementation Project

Software testing is a sport like hunting, it's bug hunting.

– **Amit Kalantri**

The purchase and implementation of the new application has been approved. The acquisition is complete, the resources are available, the project manager (PM) has been assigned, and now the implementation project can begin. As with any other project, it should follow the organization's project management methodology. Chapter 2 provided an overview of the project management framework and best practices. Organizations often tailor these standards to develop a methodology that will meet their goals, needs, and culture. While every project is unique, one that installs and configures a new application should include specific activities and tasks to ensure all requirements are included in the initial plan and met prior to the system going live. These requirements may come from organizational standards, regulatory mandates, or the specific needs of the end users. While some of these tasks may be required for each project that follows, ensuring that the application is set up correctly at the beginning is essential. In this chapter, we will discuss these additional activities and why they are important.

One of the first activities the PM should do when assigned a new project is to gather all the information currently available. In this case, there is documentation from the initial request, the analysis and the project charter or business case that was shared with the governance committee. The minutes from the governance meeting will also provide details related to their discussion, the final approval decision regarding the project scope, and any expectations related to project reporting. As was our case study, the scope of the initial request is different from what was approved. While the requestor wanted to implement the Bar Code Medication Administration (BCMA) application throughout the hospital, the decision was to implement only on the inpatient units. The remaining areas will be implemented through a separate, future project. The PM will also need to understand if the governance committee wants to review all requested changes to the scope or whether the project sponsors have the authority to make approval decisions. It is possible to have a change request (CR) be in conflict with the decision of the governance committee. It may be beneficial to bring any CRs that conflict with the scope that was approved by the committee back to them while utilizing the project sponsors for all other approval decisions.

Another source to gather information is the documentation that was used during procurement activities, which may include requirements at some level of detail. These are used to select the right application to meet the organization's needs prior to purchase. These requirements should include standards related to security, privacy, and architecture as well as user functionality. They should also be defined based on their priority, such as mandate, high priority, desired, or nice to have. While further defining the scope of the project, the PM should utilize the requirements documentation to identify which of these will be implemented or considered "In Scope" for this project. While the purchase would require the application to meet the full needs of the hospital, which may include future requirements, only the functionality specific to the inpatient areas might be included in this project. A scope statement related to this could be

1. The project will include the implementation to the ten (10) inpatient areas only. The other areas of the hospital will be implemented at a later date, in a separate project.

Project Team

The project charter identifies the resources required for the project based on the high-level scope. As the scope is refined, the list of necessary resources may need to be updated. During project planning, the required resources are assigned and the project team is formed. Below is the list of resources that may be required for the case study project and their role for the project. These will be further defined as we discuss the activities in this chapter. Please note, the titles may vary amongst organizations.

- Business Analyst – responsible for reviewing the current workflows and process flows and defining the future flows, and is also involved in defining the design of the application.
- Champion(s) – responsible for supporting the project and being the advocate for the adoption and acceptance of the change within the organization.
- Database Administrator (DBA) – responsible for installing, configuring, and maintaining all databases required for the application.
- Independent Validation and Verification (IVV) – an independent team responsible for the validation of documentation and verification of deliverables.
- Interface Team – responsible for designing and developing any integration required for this application.
- Network Administrator – responsible for evaluating the current network (wireless and wired) based on the needs of the application and its use, and updating as needed.
- Privacy Team – responsible for ensuring that the data is stored in way to maintain patient and user privacy as well as all privacy-related documentation.
- Project Manager (PM) – responsible for the overall project as it is planned, executed, and brought to a successful end.
- Post-live Support Staff – responsible for providing end user support once the project has been completed.
- Report Writer – responsible for designing and developing any reports utilized by end users or support staff.
- Security Team – responsible for ensuring security standards are configured appropriately for the application as well as all security-related testing and documentation.
- Sponsor(s) – responsible for final decisions, providing support for the PM, assistance for issue resolution, and represents the organization leadership.
- System Administrator – responsible for installing, configuring, and maintaining all servers and data center hardware.
- System Configuration Team – responsible for defining the design based on requirements, and configuring the application to meet the design.

■ Technical Architect – responsible for the overall design, integration, and implementation of the infrastructure for this application.
■ Test Team – responsible for developing test scripts and conducting testing to ensure that the requirements are met, and the system performs as designed and is ready for use.
■ Train Team – responsible for developing training materials and conducting training based on the training plan.
■ User Acceptance Testing (UAT) Team – responsible for conducting UAT, which is based on workflows and processes rather than detailed scripts.
■ User Workgroups – responsible for providing user input to the design of the application. Members of this group may be involved in UAT.

Project Stakeholders

The identification and analysis of project stakeholders begins during project initiation. The PM begins with the stakeholders that have already been identified or involved, with the request, analysis, and governance review. Speaking with these stakeholders, project team members and leadership from the impacted departments, i.e. pharmacy, nursing, and information technology (IT), will help to identify additional stakeholders. During the process of documenting the current workflow, additional stakeholders may be found. Would the scope include medications administered by physicians, respiratory therapy, or are there any medications supplied by a department other than pharmacy, such as nutritional supplements that may be provided by the dietary department? As the scope is refined, the list of stakeholders may be expanded.

A key stakeholder is the project sponsor, but there may be justification to having multiple sponsors for a single project. When implementing a new application, it could be beneficial to have a technical sponsor and a business sponsor. The technical sponsor would be a senior member of the IT department and would provide guidance and leadership for any decisions regarding the technical aspects of the project. The business sponsor would provide the same guidance and leadership for decisions related to the business aspects of the project. For our case study, there could be justification for multiple business sponsors, possibly one from the nursing department and the other from the pharmacy department. Be cautious of having too many sponsors, since this could impact their ability to make timely decisions.

The stakeholder analysis will help to identify who is impacted by the project as well as their power/authority, interest, and how they define the project's success. The PM can use this information to ensure the right communication occurs at the right time, to the right people, and in the right format. Identifying who has a positive outlook about the change being made is as important as identifying those with a negative outlook. One can assist with acceptance, while the other can hinder the project. The first can also assist with managing the second and possibly help with changing their viewpoint of the project. Once the initial stakeholder analysis is complete, there are multiple ways to display the outcomes. They can be listed in a table, as with the case study in Chapter 2, or in a matrix that identifies the communication and management levels based on their Interest and Level of Power, as with Figure 5.1. The matrix can be used with other dimensions such as Support, Influence, or Need. It is important to build a relationship with the key stakeholders and communicate appropriately with all. Remember, the stakeholder analysis is not a one-time activity; it should be reviewed and updated throughout the project. All of this information are eventually fed into the communication plan.

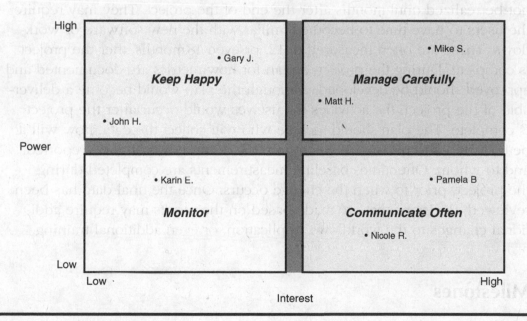

Figure 5.1   Stakeholder matrix.

Metrics

How will the success of this project be measured? There are two perspectives on what success looks like and planning for both begins during initiation. One is the evaluation of the implementation project itself. This information is used as lessons learned for the project management processes and for future projects. Frequently, one or more earned value management (EVM) metrics are used through the project to show if the project is on schedule. A listing of EVM metrics is in Appendix A. The organization determines what project success looks like and how it is measured. Is it as simple as on budget and on time, or are other metrics important, such as, meeting requirements and user acceptance? During closing, the evaluation of the project's objectives is done to provide a gap analysis between what was expected and what was delivered. The project metrics should be measured during the project and prior to releasing resources at the end.

The other perspective is the evaluation of the overall strategic goal of the project. These look at the business need and purpose of the project and if they were met. The project can be successful in relation to the metrics defined above, but if workflows and outcomes, such as patient safety, have not improved, was it really successful? Most of these evaluation activities occur outside of the project schedule. Some of these objectives may not be realized until months after the end of the project. They may require the users to have time to become familiar with the new software or workflows. These are often measured 6, 12, or even 18 months after the project is complete. During the project, a plan for how metrics are documented and approved should be developed. Although the plan would become a deliverable of the project, the activities themselves would occur after the project is complete. The plan should include who will collect the data, how will it be collected and measured, when will this occur, how will it be reported, and to whom. Oftentimes baseline measurements are completed during the project, prior to when the change occurs. Once the final data has been reviewed, decisions that are made based on the results may require additional changes to the workflows, application, or even additional training.

Milestones

The milestones for any project are developed during project planning and are based on the specific requirements, activities, and detailed tasks needed to successfully complete the project objectives. Below are examples of the milestones for our case study project. Note that some activities will occur simultaneously.

- Request Receipt and Review
- Governance Review and Approval Decision
- Architecture Review and Design
- Hardware Purchase
- Project Team Training
- Workflow and Application Design
- Hardware and Software Installation
- Application and Report Configuration
- Testing and Issue Resolution
- User Acceptance Testing
- Training Materials Developed
- Support Materials Developed
- Roll-out to Each Unit
  - Training
  - Hardware Deployed to Units
  - Activation/Go-live
  - Lessons Learned

One of the first official tasks of the project sponsor(s) is to approve the deliverables of project planning which includes the scope. The following sections will define activities involved in the initial implementation of an application organized by the project team or activity. Within the sections, scope statements will be provided for our case study project for the BCMA implementation project, and a sample scope document is provided at the end of the chapter.

Architecture

The architecture team should be involved as early in the process as possible, even before the request goes to governance for approval. The business and technical requirements should be reviewed and evaluated against any standards the organization has for applications. This evaluation should occur irrelevant irrespective to where the application will be hosted or where the data is stored. These standards may include specific operating systems or databases that the support staff has experience with, the ability to have redundancy in the case of system failure, or the ability to utilize standard integration. The architecture review will also provide insight into the cost and work effort of implementing a new system and if new hardware is required. Some applications may be able to utilize existing hardware, such as shared web server, while others require their own hardware and multiple servers. The need for additional third party software may also be identified. If the new application does not utilize the current reporting software or interface engine, obtaining, and implementing, these will need to be part of the cost and work effort. If a new application cannot meet all of the defined standards, understanding the deficiencies and the associated risks should be part of the governance discussion leading to the approval decision.

Just as would be done in the construction of a new house, the architecture needs to be defined and documented prior to any building. The architecture team should work with the vendor to define and diagram the infrastructure. This will define the gaps that will require purchasing items such as servers, workstations, printers, interface engine, or network hardware. Time for the design and purchase of any necessary hardware needs to be accommodated in the project workplan. Once the hardware arrives, it will need to be set up and configured prior to installing the new application. This will take time, but there are other tasks that can occur while waiting for the new hardware.

The architecture diagrams should define where the servers would reside in relation to any firewalls, how access is made, and any integration with other systems. The different servers are identified based on their use, such as the application server, database server, or if a web server is required. They also include how and when backups are done and any redundancy utilized for disaster recovery (DR). The pathway for the user is also diagramed out to show how they access the system and what they have access to. The design should also include the different environments that are required. Will there be a need for a development, test, and/or train environment along with production? Each of these requires separate hardware and separate instances of the application and database. While the quantity of environment is dependent on the type of system, frequency of changes, and organizational preferences, it is best practice to have at least one in addition to production to provide a location for development and validation of any changes without impacting the users. These diagrams assist with both setting up the system as well as ongoing support. They provide clear communication of the overall system and data flows.

Other items to consider while designing the application's architecture include system availability, recovery response time, what third party software should be on the server for monitoring and support, as well as where and how the application will be used. For the case study, it will be used 24 × 7 × 365, so the system needs to be up and running round the clock. With the criticality of the application, the response time for recovery would probably be the same as electronic health record (EHR). Additional software for the servers would include items such as antivirus, anti-malware, and monitoring agents.

The initial architecture design is developed in conjunction with the organization's technical resources, and the vendor and the hardware are ordered based on the approved design. While the system is being installed and configured, the design should be updated if necessary, so the documentation is accurate. During project closing, the design and documentation are finalized and shared with the support staff. A project's scope statement related to the architecture is below.

2. The initial architecture design will be documented, approved, and used for hardware purchase. The design will be updated, if necessary, during installation, and finalized during project closing.

Since the staff will probably be using wireless workstations on wheels to administer the medications at the patient's bedside, the wireless network should be evaluated. Purchasing new wireless hardware impacts the cost of the project as well as the work effort. Some of the questions to ask may include

■ Will there be increased traffic impacting the bandwidth due to an increase in the number of devices?
■ Are there dead zones where the network needs to be expanded for reliable coverage?
■ Should these devices be on their own network?

Any system integration between the BCMA application in our case study and another will also require design, development, and testing. For this project, it would be reasonable to implement a few interfaces to bring data into the BCMA and send data out. The possible interfaces could be Admission/Discharge/Transfer (ADT) inbound, Orders inbound, and Results outbound. Note that the integration is always referenced in relation to the main system in discussion, for our case study, they would be identified as inbound or outbound in relation to the BCMA system. A standard ADT interface typically includes patient demographics plus allergies, and the order interface would include all details of the medication order, and the administration details would be included as a result interface. There would also be the need for device integration between the BCMA application and the scanners, or the application used for positive patient identification. For each integration, the design should be documented, reviewed, and approved prior to any development. For interfaces between two applications, a mapping document is used. This document maps the fields from one application to the other, if it is sent directly, or if the interface engine needs to modify it. An example is if one application lists first name and last name, but the other application only uses full name, the interface engine would concatenate first and last names to send the full name. It is always best to utilize standard interfaces, if you are sending patient demographic information from the EHR to multiple other applications, using the same EHR-outbound interface where the same data is sent in the same format makes troubleshooting and maintenance easier. The scope statements related to integration may be as follows:

3. The project will include three standard interfaces with the EHR, ADT inbound, Orders Inbound and Results Outbound, and will include approved mapping documents before implementation.
4. The project will utilize the BCMA vendor's standard interface to integrate the application with the existing system used for patient identification and the handheld scanners.

Security and Privacy

As with the architecture team, the security and privacy team(s) should be involved as early as possible. There are many security and privacy controls that should be included in any and all applications. Some may be mandated by regulatory agencies while others may be required by the organization to minimize or reduce risk. It is important to note that while most people think of security and privacy together, they are different and may be separate teams in some organizations. In these cases, the information security office would be accountable for safeguarding the data from unauthorized access, while the privacy office's focus is on ensuring the confidentiality of the Protected Health Information (PHI) and the Personally Identifiable Information (PII) in the systems.

Healthcare IT systems have become a target of hackers and criminal organizations more frequently in recent years. There have been a number of high-profile attacks where information has been stolen and sold, or targeted by viruses that made the data unavailable until a ransom is paid. Healthcare systems have massive amounts of personal, private, and protected data. It is often easier, and less expensive, to include security controls during the initial implementation of the system than try to add them later.

The security and privacy standards should be included in the request analysis. There should be consistent IT requirements, based on these standards that are included in any solicitation for new software. These could range from ensuring the application can force the defined password complexity to requiring all databases can be encrypted. As with the architecture review, if a new application cannot meet all of the defined standards, understanding the deficiencies and risks should be part of the governance review and approval decision.

The security and privacy team(s) should work with the architecture team to ensure that the infrastructure design includes all the required controls prior to finalizing the design for approval. This may include the amount and placement of firewalls to ensure data security at rest and in transmission to users and other integrated systems. User access would be defined to ensure privacy of data through specific application security rights that allow access to only the information they need while restricting access to the rest. Other considerations for the infrastructure design would include items such as the options to provide security controls for local and remote access to the application. The architecture design should include all required security and privacy controls.

Once the system has been installed, there are still some security and privacy activities required prior to the system going live. Some may come from a regulatory agency or desired by the organization's standards. Either way, these should be included in the project schedule, and the PM should monitor to ensure that they are completed on time. For the case study, the scanners should be evaluated for security controls. Connected medical devices are often the weakest link in the defense of viruses and malware attacks, since they are often left unpatched or not updated. Other activities identify vulnerabilities that should be resolved. The specific activities may be dependent on the type of application, organizational requirements, and/or associated government mandates. A penetration test requires a resource with specific expertise, where the tester attempts to actively exploit any security weakness in the system. They look for pathways the hackers may use to access the application and its data. A vulnerability assessment searches for any vulnerability in the system and is often conducted through an automated tool. Any vulnerability identified from either of these tests should be evaluated and may be required to be resolved prior to the system going live.

There are a wide variety of security and privacy documentation that may be required depending on the type of organization and the type of system. Often these include the assessment of risks and issues with options to mitigate or resolve them. Other documents are agreements between organizations that define actions, or services such as remote access controls or levels of service. Your security and privacy team(s) should be able to provide the PM with a full list of what is required for each project and when they should be completed.

These security and privacy tasks and deliverables should be included in the project schedule and managed to completion. The requirements can be documented in a separate scope statement or included in others. For example, the controls related to the infrastructure would be part of the architecture design that is already included in the above scope statement. The controls for the application configuration, such as password complexity and access rights, would be included in the application requirements or design documentation so that they would be included in any scope statement related to that documentation.

Application Requirements and Design

When implementing an application that was developed by a vendor, the requirements and design decisions are different than if building a custom application. Typically, there are requirements that were documented and used for system selection during the procurement or the acquisition process. These are often listed as what the organization wants or needs the system to do. They include requirements for user functionality, security and privacy mandates, architecture standards, and support details. These requirements should be reviewed and decisions made on which will be included in the initial project and which may be implemented at a later date. One example, for our case study, could be the integration with a medication dispensing system, which is planned for the future, but not in place today. The final deliverable would be a set of requirements for this specific project. Depending on the organization's project management process, the requirements and design phase can be included in the planning or execution process group. The scope and project boundaries are approved at the end of planning. It may be important to have the approved boundaries in place prior to discussing the requirements and design to keep the focus on what will be included in the project, but that is just one option.

Before the requirements and design are discussed, the team members should learn about the new application. Vendor training to the project team will help to identify what parts of the system can be modified, options for the configuration, and how to actually do the configuration. The analyst needs to be familiar with the application and where it can be customized prior to working with the user groups to define the design. Some vendors will provide resources to assist with the design or configuration analysis, and then actually complete the configuration tasks. This is a benefit when resources are limited, but reduces the staff's knowledge when updates to the configuration are required later in the operations and maintenance phase.

Starting with the decisions on which requirements are included in the project scope and the knowledge of what parts of the application can be configured, and the configuration options, the analyst should work with the subject matter experts (SMEs) to further define the project requirements and application design. Once these are documented, the sponsor(s) would review and approve prior to any development or configuration being started. A scope statement related to these is given below. This statement is broad to limit the need for a scope change during the design activities, but clearly states there is a management review and approval step that would occur prior to beginning the next steps.

5. The application requirements and design will be documented and approved, and this will occur prior to the start of any configuration activities.

The current workflow should be documented prior to determining what the future will be. The workflow should include all steps that actually occur, not what the policies and procedures state. The documents may be old or workarounds may be in place that leads to the actual activity being different than what is documented. There are often multiple workflows in place. For example, in our case study, one would be for receiving and labeling medications by pharmacy; another would be the actual medication administration at the patient's bedside. This allows for separate meetings with the different user groups to focus on their portion of the larger process. Once the current is documented and all agree it is accurate, the future workflows can be discussed. This should include how the application and hardware will fit into the process and provide efficiencies and/or expected benefits such as improving patient safety for medication administration. Software should enhance processes, not just automate them. The future workflows should be approved by the sponsors as well and will feed into the requirements and design decisions. The scope statement for the workflow is given below.

6. The existing workflows will be evaluated and updated, as needed, by a joint working group, including nursing, pharmacy, prescribers, respiratory therapy, and IT staff. The future workflows will be documented and approved.

The vendor should be able to provide a list of all configuration options available to assist with the evaluation and decision-making activities. The evaluation of the actual application configuration options can occur anytime after team training, but some may require the application to be available. Some decisions may be easy to make, such as if the date/time format will match the EHR's format, while others are more difficult and require evaluation of the different options. The configuration of how the medication will appear when scanned at the time of administration may be best made after reviewing the different options available in the system. Actually viewing the options in the application may be necessary to properly evaluate them. This would mean the decision would need to wait until the hardware arrives and the system is fully installed. Documenting the design decisions that are required and the actual decision, once approved, feeds into the scope statement #5 above.

The security and privacy controls that are required and need to be configured into the application should also be documented and approved. These would include requirements such as the login username and password structure and the user security rights to be used. For application security rights, it is best practice to configure defined security groups with the necessary rights assigned. This makes it easier to assign users to the groups, knowing that all members of the group have the same rights. It is good to have an admin security group for those supporting the system to have additional rights for their role. These requirements would also feed into the scope statement #5 above.

Another area of configuration that is usually an afterthought is reports. The application will come with standard reports that are available. It is rare that an organization utilizes them as they are, even if the update is just to add an appropriate header and/or footer. Others may be new reports that need to be developed or the ones that require modifications to add, remove data elements, or change the formatting. It may be the report team that works to ensure that the medication labels are formatted correctly with the necessary information and the right size and type of barcode that are readable for this purpose. Modifying and developing reports is a unique skill set, and most applications utilize one of the major reporting tools, but there are others that use proprietary ones built into their application. A discussion with the report writing team will identify if additional training would be required. A scope statement for reports could be as follows.

7. The requirements for reports will be documented and approved; the scope includes development of one new report and the modification of two out-of-the-box reports.

The requirements review should also include the location for hardware such as scanners, workstations, and label printers. The future workflows will help with defining where the application will be used, so a walkthrough can be conducted to determine any gaps between the current hardware available and what is needed in each location. This may be coordinated with the technical or support staff, depending on who will be deploying the hardware. This may also identify any gaps in network access as discussed above. A scope statement for the hardware deployment could be as below.

8. The scope includes the purchase of two new label printers to be deployed into the pharmacy receiving room, and eight new scanners for patient care areas.

Once the requirements and design have been approved, any impacted documentation should be updated. These may include any policies, procedures, or new staff orientation documentation. The process for how to continue operations in the event of a system failure should also be documented. If there are already downtime procedures for the EHR, the processes for the new system could be included in that document rather than creating new.

9. The medication administration policy, procedures, and downtime processes will be updated based on the approved future workflow.

For our case study project, the PM receives a request to change the scope during the design activities. The head of the pharmacy department submitted a request to expand the implementation to all areas of the hospital, inpatient and outpatient. They felt providing medications to areas using the old and new processes would impact the workflow on pharmacy. Part of the project management plan is a document on how requested changes to any approved documents and decisions will be managed. For a requested change to the scope, the PM would work with the requestor to understand what is being requested, the purpose, and the impact if not approved. The PM would then work with the appropriate project team members to understand and document the impact the change would have to the project such as the schedule, work effort, resources, cost, and even other projects. Once the request and impact analysis is complete, the PM discusses with the sponsor(s) to receive an approval decision. They could approve, deny, or defer to a future project. For this request, the sponsors chose to defer to the governance committee since they were the ones who reduced the scope to only the inpatient areas. The governance committee denied this request since the outpatient areas could still receive medications with barcodes even if they are not scanning them during the administration. The decision would be documented and archived, but since it was denied, the scope would not require updating.

Configuration and Build

Once the decisions are made on how to configure the new application, the work can begin to make these updates. While work on the configuration of the application should wait for the design decisions to be made, work can occur simultaneously. As the decisions are made, the system can be configured. This makes the documentation of decisions more crucial, along with the importance of documenting when the configuration is made in the application. This will allow for tracking what changes have been made and which are still pending. Depending on the number of environments there are (such as with development, testing, and production), the date the change is made in each should be documented. With a new application, all configuration changes could be completed and the entire environment copied into the next, so a copy of development would be used to create a test environment. This would eliminate the need to repeat the configuration, but any changes made afterwards would need to be made in both. Typically, updates to production are made during the activation, or go-live, event. With a new application, if there isn't an impact to users, the configuration could be completed ahead of time. The activation activities will be discussed later in this chapter. With this example, Table 5.1 includes what would be documented for each decision. Some decisions do not require updates to the application, such as workflows, policies, or procedures, and in these cases "N/A" can be used, so the PM can easily see what work is still pending by looking for blanks. The decision documentation can be kept in a spreadsheet, database, or a project management tool.

Each configuration setting that is made in the application should be documented to ensure that the exact same change is made in each environment.

Table 5.1   Decision Document

Decision	Category	Final Decision	Decision-Making Authority	Date of Decision	Date Applied to Dev	Date Applied to Test	Date Applied to Prod.
What decision is needed	Used for sorting, such as workflow, documentation	The actual decision	Who made the decision (can be a group)	The date the decision was made			

This can be added to the decision documentation, kept in separate documentation or into an automated ticketing system. The documentation should include where the configuration is done, within the application, what the field name is, and the actual information entered. For our date/time example, the entry could be as below.

- Location – Configuration Tools > Global Settings > System Settings
- Field – Date Format
- Entry – MM/DD/YYYY
- Field – Time 24 hours
- Entry – Yes
- Field – Time Format
- Entry – HH:MM:SS

As with our date/time format decision, there will be some that require very little discussion before a decision can be made. These would include all mandated requirements such as the security and privacy standards. One privacy standard that may require some analysis and vendor assistance prior to the final decision would be related to the security access rights. As mentioned earlier, the use of security groups can provide efficiencies for assigning the same rights to multiple users as well as when new rights are added to the system with upgrades. Potential security groups for our case study project could be Med Admin, Pharmacist, Pharmacy Receiving, and Appl. Admin. The Med Admin group could include anyone who administers medications or you could break it down further to the user role such as nurse, physician, and respiratory therapy. Once the groups are determined, the rights available should be reviewed and applied as appropriate.

This phase also includes the development or modification of the reports defined in the scope. The development of the necessary interfaces will also be completed at this time. The scope states that standard interfaces will be used, which means that the EHR will send and receive the interface messages in a standard format that is used for all systems integrated with the EHR. The other system may ignore any data it does not need.

For our case study project, the PM received another scope CR. It was determined that the vendor cannot send the result interface messages using the expected standard format. The change and impact analysis was documented and includes the information provided in Table 5.2.

Table 5.2   Change and Impact Analysis

Project Name	BCMA Implementation
Change request #	2
Request name	Utilize custom interface for outbound results
Request description	Modify the standard result interface to include the custom elements the BCMA application requires
Request justification	The BCMA system cannot send the result interface messages in the expected format
Impact if not approved	The result interface will not be functional, and the medication administration details will not be in the EHR
Impact to work	The standard interface will need to be modified (*define what modifications are required*)
Impact to schedule	The interface modification will require 1 week, but this is not on the critical path, so the end date will not be impacted
Impact to resources	The interface team will require 24 hours of work to make the modification. The time for resolving issues was already allocated during testing
Impact to budget	No additional cost
Impact to other projects	No impact to other projects
Approval decision	Approved
Approved by	Name(s) of who approved
Date approved	Date approval decision made
Project documentation updated	Work breakdown structure (WBS) and interface mapping document

Once the CR and impact analysis is completed, it is shared with the project sponsors. Approval has been received for this request, and since the change has impacted the previously approved scope, the scope, timeline, and any other impacted project plans or documents should be updated. For tracking purposes, it is recommended to include the CR number in the statement. In our case study, this is the second CR, but the first to be approved. The new scope statement could be worded as follows:

10. Scope Change #2 – The result interface will not utilize the standard interface; it will be custom to meet the BCMA requirements. The mapping document will reflect the custom interface.

Additional items to be included during project execution would include any updates to policies or procedures. Based on the future workflow and the introduction of the new application, some non-application-specific documentation may need updating. This documentation may include those for medication administration, receiving medications in pharmacy, the preparation of medications, and their delivery to the patient care areas. If there is a downtime process in place, it should also be reviewed and updated to include when the new application is unavailable.

Testing

The testing phase is responsible for ensuring the application works as expected based on the approved requirements and configuration changes. There is a wide range of testing that could be included in a project. Chapter 2 defined the most common types of testing, unit, function/integration, regression, and acceptance testing. Other types include parallel testing where the old and new processes are used in parallel to validate the new system, performance load testing where the overall performance and response of the system is verified with the maximum user load, and interface testing where the actual interface messages are verified when sent between systems. Other activities may not be called testing, but are actually used to test or validate something. These may include the validation of the infrastructure configuration against the architecture design or even the review of the system backups to verify the nightly and incremental backups that are running as scheduled. During project planning, the test plan should be created, and it defines how testing will occur, what types of testing will be included, who will be completing the testing, when it will occur, and the documentation or deliverables to be completed.

Before testing can begin, the test team needs to be trained on how to use the application as configured. They also need to have access to the approved requirements, design decisions, future workflows, and configuration details. These documents provide the information required for building the test scripts. The test scripts are a detailed listing of each step taken to validate a requirement or configuration item, any data to be entered or selected for the test, and the expected outcome of each step. The development of test scripts can begin as soon as there are approved requirements or configuration decisions. The PM needs to ensure there is enough time in the schedule for this work, as it can take considerable time to document the test scripts for new applications when everything should be tested.

There are other preparation steps that are required prior to the beginning of the actual testing tasks. There should be a specific environment used for testing. This could be the same one used for development, or a separate controlled environment. Changes to the test environment should be controlled to avoid unintended impacts to the testing outcomes. The development and test environments should not include any real patient data. Fake, or test, data should be used, which requires the entry or loading of this data prior to the beginning of any testing. Once the security groups are configured, a test account can be added to each group so the specific access can be verified, and each test script should identify which account(s) should be used to ensure access to the correct functionality is available. As each item is tested, any issues should be reported to the PM and tracked. The issue will be assigned for evaluation and eventual resolution. Although the issue may be assigned to another resource, the PM is still responsible for ensuring it gets resolved. Once resolved, the issue remains open until it is retested. During retesting of an issue, it is important to follow the exact same test script using the exact same data. This will eliminate any possible variability based on steps or data that could have caused the issue and verifies what was seen originally is resolved. The issues list would include the final test scripts (original and retest), the analysis outcome, and the steps for resolution along with all appropriate dates. The project schedule should include the time to resolve and retest any testing issues as this is often forgotten, which results in project delays.

Once all testing has been completed and issues have been resolved, UAT can be scheduled. As mentioned in Chapter 2, you only have one opportunity to make a first impression, so ensuring that the system is fully tested by the test team prior to this step is critical. The UAT is conducted with scripts that are less detailed than the other testing methods. These are more workflow and functionality focused. The test script may list high-level tasks based on the new workflows rather than the detailed steps. Because the detailed steps are not listed, the UAT resources will need to be trained on how to use the application. This requires the training materials to be completed at least in a final draft form. This step also provides a validation of the training materials prior to finalizing them and beginning end user training. Any issues found during this testing activity should be documented separately from the rest of the test issues. Often these issues can be categorized into critical, future enhancement, or training. Critical issues are actual problems with the applications that require resolution before the go-live date. These should be added to the issues list and managed through to resolution and validation. Future enhancements are items that are not issues with the system, but may include comments about changes in functionality and how the system looks. They are not in scope, or it is unclear if the change would be acceptable beyond the person doing the testing. These are listed and evaluated at a later date and, if approved, are implemented outside of this project. Training issues are the ones that were identified simply because the tester did not know how to do the step or action. These should be reported to the training team to be evaluated for updating their training materials. The UAT result documentation should include the list of all issues, the category, and the final outcome. A scope statement related to testing could be as follows.

11. All testing will be completed and critical issues resolved prior to the system activation.

At any time after the infrastructure has been set up and the production environment is available, the security team will conduct the penetration test as identified above in the security and privacy section. The timing of this test should allow for the resolution of vulnerabilities prior to the go-live date. Once all the testing is complete, the test team can focus on developing regression test scripts. These are limited scripts that include key functionality of the application and are used to confirm future changes do not have any adverse effects on the existing functionality.

Training

The training phase is responsible for ensuring all users are knowledgeable on the functionality of the application, and any updated policies, procedures, and/or workflows prior to using it. As with testing, the training plan begins during project planning and outlines what training will be provided, what format will be used, what materials will be required, as well as when and where training will be conducted. The case study project's implementation plan has the application being rolled out one unit at a time with training occurring during this schedule. This provides a guide on who should be trained and what the timeline would be. The location for training should allow enough space for the estimated class size along with the necessary materials. If training is conducted as a demonstration and discussion, the space can be smaller if hands-on exercises will be used requiring a workstation and scanner for each user. The training plan should also include if the vendor will train the project team prior to their tasks, including the UAT resources. The plan should also address the vendor's involvement in the training of end users. Often the training of support staff is part of the transition to support activities, but these training materials and space could be used for that training as well.

This may be the first time the end users have seen the new application or logged into the application, so training must start with the very basics. How will the application be accessed, will there be an icon on the workstation's desktop, and what login credentials do they use? Some training can be provided through written materials and general communication, while more complex functionality may require a demonstration followed by hands-on exercises.

No matter how the training is provided, it is best practice to provide training based on the user's role within the system. This teaches them only the functionality they have access to and will use. The training plan should define the types of training to be provided across the different user groups. Will training be provided by functionality, such as access, medication administration, medication management (pharmacy updating the medications in the system), or will it be by user type, such as pharmacy, nursing, and physicians? The first option would require users to take multiple classes depending on how they will use the system; the second option will require duplication of training for the different groups. These decisions will impact the training materials required. The training could also include a quick reference guide for the users to take with them after training. This can help with remembering some of the basics of the new application. The training materials can be reused in the future for new employees when hired.

As with testing, training should not be conducted using real patient data. Will there be justification for a separate training environment due to the volume of training being provided? Training data will need to be loaded into the environment that will be used. This data should match up with the training materials so the user is able to view the expected information as defined in the materials as training progresses. This is especially important if practice exercises will be used to ensure the right information is available for the student to complete the task in the exercise. A process for refreshing the data in the training environment should be put into place if the students will be making changes during the class by way of exercises. This will refresh the data back to the way it was before the class, so the next student can complete the same exercise.

The training materials, environment, and data refresh practices should remain in place for training new employees as they are hired. These should also be updated as any changes are made to the application during operations and maintenance.

Configuration and Release Management

After the testing is completed, there should be a standard process for how any changes are made. These changes must be managed to ensure they are approved, tested, and included in all environments. Configuration management (CM) defines how these changes will be made; both after testing is complete during the project as well as how the changes are made after the application is live. The process relates to any changes to the system, which includes the application, infrastructure, and integration. Release management (RM) refers to the process of releasing the changes to the different environments. CM and RM are further defined in Chapter 7.

During the project, these processes need to be defined and communicated. If there is already a process in place for other applications, such as the EHR, they can be updated to include this application. This is the best option for consistency of changes across all applications in the portfolio. There should be a period of time just before the go-live date where no changes are made. This is called "Code Freeze," which allows the system to be fully tested, stable, and eliminates the risk of the adverse effects of last-minute changes. The code freeze could be any defined length of time, but should be at least 1 week. There should also be a delay between when the system goes live and when new CRs will be accepted. This is to allow the users to become familiar with the application and new workflow prior to asking for updates to get the application to match the old workflow. This is typically 1–3 months. Any reported issues with the application should be resolved as they are identified.

Go-Live Planning: Rollout Process (Deploying)

Decisions made during project planning will impact the activation or go-live. The implementation plan is a big influencer on the activation, but the other plans will also affect what happens during this activity. As with other portions of the project, planning for the activation should occur early in the project to ensure that all stakeholders are prepared for the day the new application is live. Activation planning is more than just how to turn the system on; it involves all activities just before, during, and just after the actual go-live.

The actual tasks involved will vary greatly based on the project. Some projects require a period of time when an application is unavailable, such as the migration of a legacy application to a new one or with an upgrade of a current application. In these situations, there are many decisions to be made, starting with when is the best time for the system to be unavailable, that will have the least impact on operations. How will the operations continue without the application should also be evaluated? A business continuity plan or downtime procedure should be put into place, or reviewed and updated as needed. Communication of the plan should occur to all impacted users, and if possible, demonstration or rehearsal of the plan could occur.

Chapter 2 describes the use of a sticky-note meeting to develop the activation checklist. This checklist should include all tasks that are required for the activation, even if they occur prior or after the actual go-live date. Once the initial checklist is created, the activation team should meet to review it. Each review meeting provides the opportunity to refine the checklist, and the PM should allow enough time for multiple reviews, especially if the checklist is a new concept for the team. Once there is a solid checklist that has been fully reviewed and all agree it is as accurate as possible, a rehearsal should be scheduled. The rehearsal is beneficial to ensure everyone is aware of their tasks and how to complete them, validates the tasks on the checklist, and helps to identify the expected duration of the downtime, if any. Having a checklist displayed on a screen allows the entire team to view the progress and if the activity is ahead or behind schedule. An additional resource that may be brought in for the activation is a checklist manager. This person would manage the checklist, informing staff when to begin their tasks and updates the checklist as the work progresses. This leaves the PM available for activities such as managing issues and communication. During the rehearsal, the actual start and end times for each task are documented as well as any missing tasks or moving tasks around if they are out of order. Afterwards, the rehearsal is discussed to understand if there are any lessons to be learned as well as to review the checklist to finalize it for activation.

When creating the checklist there are a number of tasks that should be considered. Will there be the need to migrate data? This is used when replacing a legacy application with something new or when there is a need to prepopulate the new application. If this is completely new, as with our case study, will there be a need to load data from the EHR such as patient demographics, medication orders, and allergies. All users will need to be added to the new application either manually or through a data load. They will also require the assignment of their security access through groups or individual security rights. To keep users off the application before it is ready they may need to be kept inactive until it is live. If this is the case, there should be a task on the checklist to activate the users. These are just some of the questions the PM should ask when developing the checklist.

For the case study, the activation may not be as complex. This is a new system, and the users are moving from a process where they are documenting in the EHR to using the new application to scan barcodes for the verification and administration of medications. There may not be a need for any downtime of the EHR or BCMA system, and the majority of the tasks may be completed in advance. With the implementation plan for rolling the new application out one inpatient unit at a time, the plan should be to have the system fully ready when the first unit goes live. So the initial activation activities would include adding all users and all updates of the production environment with the approved configuration that passed testing, and for the first unit, training, loading the patient data, and activating the users. The rollout plan would have support staff on the unit post-live, while repeating the steps to loading data, activating users, and training the next unit prior to their activation.

The PM should have a plan for reporting issues during the immediate time postlive. If the organization already has a help desk, this would be a good option for documenting and tracking issues as they are identified. Another option is to use support staff on the unit, if this is part of the postlive plan. They could collect issues as well as provide just-in-time training, or "how to" assistance, when needed. The issues should be documented and categorized and, anything identified as critical, should be assigned and managed through to resolution. These fixes should follow the CM process and be fully tested before being put into production. As with the UAT, the other categories could be future enhancement and training. A few days after each unit goes live, the team should come together to discuss any lessons learned from that activation. While project lessons learned can be documented, the purpose of these meetings is to identify any opportunities for improvement for the next unit activation.

In our case study project, as the project team prepares for the activation in the intensive care unit (ICU), the nurse manager requests a delay in the activation due to high census. The unit is full and acuity is higher than normal requiring additional staffing. The scope CR is to delay the activation until the outpatient units go live. The PM has reviewed the request and documented the impact analysis. Upon bringing this request to the project sponsor(s) there is not an agreement on the final decision. The CR was deferred to the governance committee. The governance committee approved the request to be completed as soon as the census drops to 75% capacity. This may be before the outpatient areas or the first unit to go live during that project. The associated scope statement would be

12. The ICU will not be included in this project and will be added to the scope of the following outpatient project.

Post-Live Support

It is not uncommon for the project team to remain the primary point of contact for any postlive issues for a few weeks. This keeps the team resources available for any immediate issues that may arise during this time. The size, complexity, and criticality of the application will impact how long the project team should remain in the support role. The project should not be closed until the support is transitioned to the help desk or support staff. The planning for this transition begins during project planning and requires documentation, communication, and education to the support staff as well as communication to the users on how to get help after the project is over. The transition to support is further discussed in Chapter 6.

Project Closing

Once the objectives of the project have been met and the unique product or service has been delivered, it is time to close out the project. Chapter 2 identifies a variety of activities that occur during this phase of the project, including collecting and documenting lessons learned, and finalizing the issues and risk lists. The after action report, or completion document, was referenced in Chapter 2, where it notes that the PM must be able to state definitively whether the objectives were met. The report is a type of gap analysis between the original plan, and any approved changes, to what actually occurred during the project. It identifies if all scope statements were met, including any approved scope changes, and if not why. The list of these statements is included in the example of a full completion document at the end of this chapter, after the scope document.

This report should also include any comments on the assumptions and constraints to note if their impact was as expected. The project metrics should be finalized and if any measures of success were noted, they should be reviewed. Once this after action report is complete, it should be reviewed with the sponsors and signed off to show their acceptance of the project completion.

Throughout any project, the application list should be updated with all necessary details. The PM should verify whether the application was added to the list when the approval decision was made, or add it if not. As the project progresses and the details are defined, they should be added. During the closing phase, all contents should be reviewed to ensure they are complete and accurate based on the system when it went live. This should include the baseline configuration that will be referenced by the team during operations and maintenance activities.

All project plans should be reviewed and finalized based on the status at the end of the project. Once all documentation is finalized, they should be archived so that they are available for future projects as historical information. At this time, remember to celebrate the successful end of the project prior to releasing all resources, including the PM.

Bar Code Medication Administration: Scope

Purpose/Mission Statement

The BCMA application will automate error-resistant patient care processes to improve efficiency, effectiveness, and patient safety for medication administration. The barcode-enabled, automated point-of-care technology solution is intended to address hospital-wide processes for medication administration and to integrate with the existing barcode technologies for positive patient identification. The application shall provide the ability to support the medication administration process, including verification of the right patient, right drug, right dose, right strength, right time and right route of administration, and clinical reason as appropriate. BCMA involves the commitment of prescriber, pharmacist, nurse, and patient to a safer and more efficient process surrounding the medication function.

Objectives/Scope Statements

1. The project will include the implementation to the ten (10) inpatient areas only. The other areas of the hospital will be implemented at a later date, in a separate project.
2. The initial architecture design will be documented, approved, and used for hardware purchase. The design will be updated, if necessary, during installation, and finalized during project closing.
3. The project will include three standard interfaces with the EHR, ADT inbound, Orders Inbound and Results Outbound, and will include approved mapping documents before implementation.
4. The project will utilize the BCMA vendor's standard interface to integrate the application with the existing system used for patient identification and the handheld scanners.
5. The application requirements and design will be documented and approved, and this will occur prior to the start of any configuration activities.
6. The existing workflows will be evaluated and updated, as needed, by a joint working group, including nursing, pharmacy, prescribers, respiratory therapy, and IT staff. The future workflows will be documented and approved.

7. The requirements for reports will be documented and approved; the scope includes development of one new report and the modification of two out-of-the-box reports.
8. The scope includes the purchase of two new label printers to be deployed into the pharmacy receiving room and eight new scanners for patient care areas.
9. The medication administration policy, procedures, and downtime processes will be updated based on the approved future workflow.
10. All testing will be completed and critical issues resolved prior to the system activation.

Justification

To improve patient safety related medication administration

Implementation Strategy

BCMA will be implemented one inpatient unit at a time. Subsequent units will be rolled out one every 2 weeks, in the order approved by the sponsor.

Training Strategy

The vendor will provide a Train the Trainer session to the nursing and pharmacy superusers who will then provide end user training. The training will be conducted for each inpatient unit prior to the activation, in the order they will be implemented.

Communication Plan

The PM will conduct a weekly status meeting throughout the duration of the project and the minutes will be distributed to the team and sponsors via email. Additional meetings may be conducted on an ad hoc basis to discuss specific issues related to the project. Issues needing escalation should be brought to the PM as soon as possible.

Audience	What	When	How	Responsible Party
Sponsor	• Project status • Escalated issues	• Barcode leadership meeting • As needed	Email Verbal – phone call or recorded in minutes	Project manager
Project Management Office (PMO)	Project status	Monthly	Project list spreadsheet	Project manager
Project manager	• Status on work accomplished • Risks or issues • Decisions affecting the project	Weekly Monthly	Verbal – recorded in minutes Email	All project team members
Project team	• Testing requirements and issues • Testing results	Before, during, and after testing	Written reports Verbal – recorded in minutes Test plan	Test team lead
Project team	• Tasks • Decisions • Info about other projects that impact this one • Risks and issue status	Weekly	Verbal – recorded in minutes	Project manager
End users	Training	Ad hoc activation	To Be Determined (TBD)	Trainers

Project Milestones

Milestone	Estimated Completion Date
Workflow and design decisions complete	
Application configuration complete	
Application testing complete	
Rollout of Unit	
Additional hardware deployed	
End users training complete	
Activation	
Rollout of Additional Units	
Lessons learned meeting	
Additional hardware deployed	
End user training complete	
Activation	

Operations and Maintenance (O&M)

- The IT department will manage the maintenance of the infrastructure and the hardware on the units (computers, carts, and scanners).
- Pharmacy will manage the maintenance of the medication barcodes and their configuration within the application.
- Any requested changes to the system will be managed following the same CM and RM process followed for the EHR.

Measures of Success

- All medications have available barcodes
- All impacted staff are aware of and utilize the new workflows
- The BCMA is integrated with the barcode patient identification system
- The BCMA is integrated with the EHR
- The project is successfully completed once all units are "up" with BCMA

Constraints

A list of items that could prevent this project from moving forward as planned (related to risks)

- Computers do not have access to the BCMA client
- No integration between the barcode patient identification system and the BCMA system
- Unreliable integration between the EHR and BCMA
- Weak wireless strength/unreliable connectivity where needed on the patient care units

Assumptions

A list of items that are assumed to be true, have taken place, or will be provided for the project to move forward as planned.

- The new workflows are adopted by all stakeholders
- The application configuration supports the approved workflows
- A lessons learned meeting will be held after each unit goes live to "learn" for the next unit being implemented
- Two weeks is enough time between unit implementations, to complete all necessary work.

Project Team

Project Sponsor(s):
Project Manager:
Project Resources:

Approvals

_____   _____

Sponsor   Date

_____   _____

Sponsor   Date

_____   _____

Project Manager   Date

Bar Code Medication Administration: Completion Document

Purpose/Mission Statement

The BCMA application will automate error-resistant patient care processes to improve efficiency, effectiveness, and patient safety for medication administration. The barcode-enabled, automated point-of-care technology solution is intended to address hospital-wide processes for medication administration and to integrate with the existing barcode technologies for positive patient identification. The application shall provide the ability to support the medication administration process, including verification of the right patient, right drug, right dose, right strength, right time and right route of administration, and clinical reason as appropriate. BCMA involves the commitment of prescriber, pharmacist, nurse, and patient to a safer and more efficient process surrounding the medication function.

Objectives/Scope Statements

1. The project will include the implementation to the ten (10) inpatient areas only. The other areas of the hospital will be implemented at a later date, in a separate project.
   - Met – CR #3 removes the ICU from scope – all other areas were implemented
2. The initial architecture design will be documented, approved, and used for hardware purchase. The design will be updated, if necessary, during installation, and finalized during project closing.
   - Met – the final architecture design is available *HERE*
3. The project will include three standard interfaces with the EHR, ADT inbound, Orders Inbound and Results Outbound, and will include approved mapping documents before implementation. (See CR #2 below)
   - Met – CR #2 updates the result interface to be custom and all others are standard.
4. The project will utilize the BCMA vendor's standard interface to integrate the application with the existing system used for patient identification and the handheld scanners.
   - Met

5. The application requirements and design will be documented and approved, and this will occur prior to the start of any configuration activities
   - Met – the approved requirements and design are available *HERE*
6. The existing workflows will be evaluated and updated, as needed, by a joint working group including nursing, pharmacy, prescribers, respiratory therapy, and IT staff. The future workflows will be documented and approved.
   - Met – the workflows were documented and approved. They were also incorporated in the UAT scripts and training materials.
7. The requirements for reports will be documented and approved; the scope includes the development of one new report and the modification of two out-of-the-box reports.
   - Met – the approved requirements are available *HERE*
8. The scope includes the purchase of two new label printers to be deployed into the pharmacy receiving room, and eight new scanners for patient care areas.
   - Met – purchased and deployed as planned
9. The medication administration policy, procedures, and downtime processes will be updated based on the approved future workflow.
   - Met – new policies and procedures in place and communicated.
10. Change Request #2 – The result interface will not utilize the standard interface, and it will be custom to meet the BCMA requirements
    - Met – see scope statement #3 above
11. All testing will be completed and critical issues resolved prior to the system activation.
    - Met
12. Change Request #3 – The ICU will not be included in this project and will be added to the scope of the following outpatient project.
    - Met – see scope statement #1 above, new project request created for the ICU implementation.

Implementation Strategy

BCMA will be implemented one inpatient unit at a time. Subsequent units will be rolled out one every 2 weeks, in the order approved by the sponsor.

The implementation strategy was followed with the exception of the ICU, which was taken out of scope with CR #3.

Training Strategy

The vendor will provide a Train the Trainer session to the nursing and pharmacy superusers who will then provide end user training. The training will be conducted for each inpatient unit prior to the activation, in the order they will be implemented.

The training strategy was followed, and the affected prescribers were included in the nursing end user training which was renamed Medication Administration training.

Communication Plan

The PM will conduct a weekly status meeting throughout the duration of the project and the minutes will be distributed to the team and sponsors via email. Additional meetings may be conducted on an ad hoc basis to discuss specific issues related to the project. Issues needing escalation should be brought to the PM as soon as possible.

Communication was conducted per the defined plan. Ad hoc meetings included the user workgroup that assisted with workflow redesign.

Project Milestones

Milestone	Actual Completion Date
Workflow and design decisions complete	
Application configuration complete	
Application testing complete	
Activation unit 1	
Activation unit 2	
Activation unit 3	
Activation unit 4	
Activation unit 5	
Activation unit 6	
Activation unit 7	
Activation unit 8	
Activation unit 9	

Measures of Success

- All medications have available barcodes
  - Met prior to unit 1 activation
- All impacted staff are aware of and utilize the new workflows
  - Met through communication at multiple unit meetings, prior to their activation, to ensure all staff are aware. Post-live support on each unit helped to verify new workflows were utilized.
- The BCMA is integrated with the barcode patient identification system
  - Met prior to unit 1 activation
- The BCMA is integrated with the EHR
  - Met prior to unit 1 activation
- Project is successfully completed once all units are "up" with BCMA
  - Met for all inpatient units, except ICU (CR #3)

Constraints

- Computers do not have access to the BCMA client
  - All identified computers that will be used by BCMA were verified to have a working client installed
- No integration between the barcode patient identification system and the BCMA system
  - The integration was successful and verified
- Unreliable integration between the EHR and BCMA
  - The integration was successful and verified
- Weak wireless strength/unreliable connectivity where needed on the patient care units
  - The network survey identified a few wireless dead zones that were resolved with the installation of additional access points.

Assumptions

- The new workflows are adopted by all stakeholders
  - The workflows are being adopted, there were some who were resistant to change, but the sponsors and organizational leadership assisted with communicating the need for adoption.
- The application configuration supports the approved workflows
  - This was verified through UAT as each unit went live.

- A lessons learned meeting will be held after each unit goes live to "learn" for the next unit being implemented
  - The lessons learned meetings were held within 4 days of each unit's activation and initially provided many opportunities for improvement. By the last few units, there were minimal, if any, lessons identified.
- Two weeks is enough time between unit implementations, to complete all necessary work.
  - For the first few, we expanded to every 3 weeks due to the quantity of opportunities for improvement, but by the fourth unit, the schedule was back to every 2 weeks.

Lessons learned can be found *HERE*

Approvals

_____   _____

Sponsor   Date

_____   _____

Sponsor   Date

_____   _____

Project Manager   Date

Chapter 6

Transition to Support

> This is the greatest and most fraught romance of modern society,
> the marriage between the IT staff and those who depend on them.
>
> **– Marilyn Johnson**
> *This Book is Overdue! How Librarians*
> *and Cybrarians Can Save Us All*

A successful information technology (IT) department will never have a lack of new requests from their stakeholders, especially when it comes to the implementation of new healthcare applications and patient care solutions. Even everyday devices, such as freezers, may include temperature-monitoring systems that interface with other systems in the hospital. It can be expected that IT projects will only become more complex, take longer to complete, and cost more to implement. As applications are introduced to the hospital's portfolio, the toll on existing IT staff will intensify, as they attempt to maintain a balance between supporting existing systems while meeting the new demands of the organization. As we all know, human resources and financial budgets are not unlimited, so there must be appropriate planning throughout the project lifecycle to anticipate the ongoing support needs of each new and modified application. This planning must go beyond the idea of throwing some job aids and knowledge base articles at a support center and should be an integral part of the application implementation process. This chapter will provide a detailed guide on how to develop a plan to transition projects to successful operations and maintenance processes.

As we learned at the beginning of this book, projects are not open-ended concepts and should be treated as temporary endeavors. Likewise, at the conclusion of the project, all resources should be released from the requirements of the objectives, including the project manager (PM). While this makes logical sense, it can be challenging for some organizations to separate the PM from the application that he or she implemented. After all, the PM was responsible for the day-to-day workload and likely had a firm grasp of every aspect of the project work. If an issue was uncovered, the PM knew who it should be assigned to and how to escalate it to make sure it was resolved. If there was a need for changes, the PM served as the central figure to assist with change management documentation and approvals. And if there were ever any questions from staff, customers, or executives, they knew they could count on the PM to provide answers in a quick and effective manner. It's easy to fall into this trap, as well. The best PMs have excellent personalities and can successfully network with stakeholders throughout an organization. They also have a strong sense of customer satisfaction and are likely to do whatever is needed to ensure timely resolution of issues and questions. At the same time, the customers that have grown accustomed to working with the PM will see them as the best resource for getting the information they need.

So, what's the harm in adding a little more workload to the PM to make sure customers are happy? Or, allowing them to become the escalation point when other processes aren't working? After all, it seems like a win–win: The customers get what they need, and the PM is able to deliver on their desire for customer service. The problem stems from the idea that the number of IT requests is growing exponentially and are becoming more complex. If PMs were expected to provide support on old projects, no matter how limited, each new application they implement would start to cut into their total available time. They would quickly start spending more of their workday managing existing products instead of implementing new ones, creating an increased backlog of new requests. Or, if they are directed to focus on new projects and a proper handoff hasn't taken place, there is a higher likelihood that customer service will fall short of expectations on the support of older applications. Additionally, and perhaps more critically, it can create a risky perception that PMs are better equipped to handle support issues than the IT department itself. This type of thinking will likely snowball into a situation of department infighting, lack of trust between different IT groups, decreased employee morale, and problems with retaining effective staff.

The solution is twofold: (1) Ensuring that your organization has an effective and appropriate support process in place and (2) Integrating a transition process into every phase of the project lifecycle.

Developing a Support Process

Before a PM can consider transitioning an application from project phase to support phase, there obviously must be some support process already in place. The requirements for a strong support system include

1. Aligning the number of resources to the workload
2. Developing a strong, centralized support center
3. Identifying product/application owners
4. Obtaining buy-in from executive leadership

Aligning the Number of Resources to the Workload

Optimally, an organization would have a set of dedicated staff that are responsible for the ongoing care and feeding of applications, and their role would not intersect with the implementation of new systems. Likewise, each new system implementation would include the addition of new, permanent employees to support the new application. While this may be feasible when enterprise-wide systems are implemented, most organizations cannot justify the continued expansion of the IT department for each new application that's added to the portfolio. This has created a situation where more and more organizations are reliant upon the same individual(s) to assist with the implementation of new applications, while still trying to support those that are already in place. At some point, the IT department will reach capacity for support, and that line can be very difficult to measure. After all, no one wants to be perceived as being a failure, and most organizations have well-meaning employees that will continue to take on more work to meet the mission of the organization. The impact of these increased responsibilities goes beyond the moaning and groaning that can be expected with overal-located resources. There are some key indicators that should be viewed as flags to executive leadership that increased resources in the IT department are needed, including (1) An increase in the amount of overtime being requested; (2) A decrease in the quality of work outputs from typically high-performing individuals; (3) Exceptionally long project durations, or projects that are consistently missing expected deadlines; (4) Staff burnout, leading to higher than normal turnover rates; and (5) An overall feeling from staff that they are working harder but have less to show for their efforts.

Organizations that are demonstrating these warning signs of overal-location should immediately begin to review their workflow processes and ensure that resources are properly aligned to workload. There are basically two strategies to consider: Either increasing the available resources to complete the work (more money) or decreasing the work that needs to be performed (saying no). Either option will come at a cost, but the risk of underperforming on the majority of projects will have a greater impact on the long-term efficiency and effectiveness of the IT department.

The first step in deciding how to approach resource alignment is to determine what staff are doing with their time. This may seem like an obvious question or one where executives will mutter, "Well, if the managers don't know what their staff is doing, we have an even bigger problem on our hands." But the truth is that it can be difficult to pin down exactly what everyone is doing at any given time. Managers need to consider that even if they have staff that are 100% dedicated to a specific effort, that doesn't necessarily mean that they are spending 40 hours a week on that work. As we reviewed in Chapter 4, staff still need to divide their time between assigned work, general administrative tasks, staff meetings, unplanned emergencies, training, analysis of upcoming tasks, operational work, and (gasp) taking snack breaks or having occasional personal conversations with fellow colleagues. Performing an analysis of activities across all staff may be a good way to begin to understand the current workload.

Historical timesheets and conversations with front-line managers is a good starting point, but it's unlikely that staff will admit to doing any work other than the specific tasks that they have been assigned to complete. Performing a *time and motion study* could garner the additional details needed. This is typically performed by an external observer, who monitors the workload of staff and documents how they are spending their day. Although it may seem more accurate than self-reporting, most people do not want someone hovering over their desk all day. There are also automated tracking tools available that require staff to clock in and out of different activities or applications. Some tools even incorporate wearable tracking devices to determine when employees are at their desk and when they are in the field. Regardless of the method used, involving the employee in the process is crucial. They need to understand how the data is going to be used and know that these studies are meant to narrow the focus of the department and increase the value of what each employee brings to the table.

Once this information is gathered, there also needs to be an understanding of the workload being requested of the department. This should start with every new and pending request given to the department. Once an analyst has completed their work on the development of a business case or project charter, there should be enough information available to identify the teams that need to be involved in the work and a high-level estimate of the amount of time they will spend on that project. There cannot be an expectation of accurate numbers until the project has started and planning is complete, but providing estimates early on will help the organization understand the impact of starting one project versus another (or versus the current workload). These are a few strategies for providing these estimates:

1. **Comparison to similar projects:** This may be particularly useful for vendors who implement their applications time and again in multiple hospitals. Although the specific requirements may differ, the overall process for implementation is similar, and they can plan out their resources accordingly. Hospital IT departments may not be so lucky, as each project may have radically different objectives from one another. However, there should be some similarities. For example, most new application implementations may include reviews and documentation from security and privacy teams, and those processes are unlikely to change dramatically from one project to another. Therefore, if you know that an application needs to undergo those reviews, you can create a project template with the estimated resources, tasks, and timelines that can be plugged into the new request. Similar templates could be derived from those in the system administration team or the testing team or the interface and integration teams. Once you have a good baseline for how long these tasks will take, you can provide a much better estimate based on the specific objectives of the new project request.

2. **Provide a complexity score:** Chapter 4 described a weighted scoring technique that can be used to identify the difficulty or work effort of new requests. That score can be used to determine the overall complexity of the request, which can then be multiplied by the standard time that was derived through the comparison to other similar projects.

3. **Input from impacted teams:** Once the baseline hours for a project have been determined, that information can be shared with the leads of each team to confirm or modify the anticipated workload, as appropriate. Sharing this information early allows those managers to plan their staff time while also feeling like they are contributing to the strategic direction of the department.

Table 6.1   Resource-to-Project Allocation

Project Due to Start in the Next 3 Months	Impact Score	IT Department Team Hours						
		PM	System Admin	Database Admin	Build Team	Interface Team	Testing Team	Work Effort by Project
Health record upgrade	4.2	575	120	680	425	100	300	2,200
Data center migration	4.1	400	600	40	0	0	75	1,115
Lab system replacement	3.0	350	100	75	200	80	100	905
Clin. doc. rebuild	2.2	100	0	0	450	0	200	750
Genetic pedigree	3.1	150	50	75	400	0	250	925
Work Effort by Team	X	1,575	870	870	1,475	180	925	5,895

If this process is repeated for all inbound requests, the IT department can compile that data into a matrix, which will provide a higher level of confidence in the anticipated workload of the department in the coming months. An example of this matrix is shown in Table 6.1.

In the table above, projects that are slated to start in the next 3 months are shown, along with the total estimated commitment by team. However, since the work effort will ebb and flow throughout the duration of a project, a more detailed analysis on a quarter-by-quarter or month-by-month basis could be created, as demonstrated in Table 4.3 of Chapter 4. By taking both the capacity and demand information, you can create a stacked chart to visually show how work requirements impact staff capacity (Figure 6.1).

In this example, even though new project work and operational activities consistently fall below the staff capacity line, when you consider the time spent performing administrative and other work-related duties, the total capacity for the team or department becomes overallocated. By providing this level of detail to governance boards or hospital leadership, the IT department can have a higher level of confidence in presenting their case for additional resources or fewer concurrent projects.

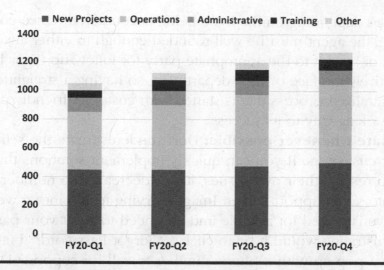

Figure 6.1   Capacity vs. demand.

Developing a Strong, Centralized Support Center

Despite the best efforts of senior management to present the case for more people, the likelihood of the IT department getting all the resources they need to successfully and permanently separate the tasks of implementation vs. maintenance may not be realistic. However, the constant interruption of work due to the issue of the day or routine firefighting can have a negative impact on the overall productivity of the team. Therefore, the key is to lessen the burden by reducing the number of interruptions, especially when the support tasks are simple or repetitive, such as answering how-to questions or creating user accounts. The solution is to create a strong, centralized support center, such as a help desk or self-service application. By taking the initial burden of answering initial inquiries from customers, it's possible that most of the initial calls can be solved quickly without having to interfere with the workload of project staff. The help desk does not need to be a formal hub where a bunch of employees are sitting together in half cubicles with headsets using fancy software. Something as simple as a single shared phone number or a common distribution list can do the trick. Regardless of the input method, there are a few attributes of a successful support center that will drive customer and employee satisfaction:

1. **Keep the process simple:** From the customer's standpoint, there should be a single, centralized method for requesting support. You cannot expect the customer to search for different phone numbers or email

addresses depending on the issue being encountered. Once contact is made, the agent must be well-rounded enough to either answer the inquiry or send it to the appropriate party for follow-up. Your help desk is effectively the face of your department, so having a straightforward and centralized process that is staffed with customer-friendly personnel will go a long way to its success.

2. **Automate whenever possible:** Don't underestimate the self-reliance of your customers. If you can quickly implement solutions that allow users to resolve their own issues, it will decrease the number of calls into your support center. Imagine trying to log into a web site you haven't visited for a while and you need to reset your password. How frustrating would it be to click a "Forgot Password?" button and receive a pop-up with a phone number to call for support? Don't be afraid to give customers the ability to perform routine functions for themselves.

3. **Aim to resolve calls at first contact:** We all know how frustrating it can be when we call a company, just to spend a half hour on hold, get punted from one agent to another, and then have the line disconnected. Keeping your support center up to date on new project implementations or changes to workflow processes can help provide agents with the information they need to know.

4. **Escalate issues, as appropriate:** It's important to strike a balance between providing enough information for your agents to know what they are talking about yet avoid drowning them in a myriad of knowledge articles and job aids. If they need to put their caller on hold for more than a few minutes to find the information they need, they either have too much documentation on the subject, or it's time to hand off the call to an escalation point. Creating a tiered structure between agent, subject matter expert, and programmer/builder helps to get the right information to the customer while limiting the calls that end up with the highest tier level.

5. **Create a collaborative environment:** Despite the need to establish tiered support levels, it's important to make sure that help desk agents do not feel like they are at the bottom of the totem pole, nor should those at the highest level get a sense of undue entitlement. Personnel issues should be handled quickly, and it should never be acceptable for internal problems to be voiced to the customer. Everyone from the ground-up must feel a sense that they are contributing to the success of the support center and the organization as a whole.

6. **Monitor the support center performance:** Keeping tabs on the types of issues being reported, how they are handled, and how customers react to the process is an important part of keeping the support center running smoothly. Look for trends of commonly reporting issues or questions that can either be fixed or automated. If too many calls are escalated, it's possible that more agent documentation or training is needed. If agents are not treating customers with appropriate levels of respect, perhaps there may be other opportunities for that agent to pursue.

Identifying Product/Application Owners

When customer issues are identified through the support system, it's important for the IT teams to understand the difference between something that is not working (break/fix) and something that is a change to the underlying functionality of the system. System changes can have dramatic and unintended effects on workflow processes. Even renaming a field or moving it from one place to another without proper communication can create confusion and frustration on the part of the end user. Additionally, there may be situations where an issue or change needs to be escalated or monitored to ensure a successful resolution. However, once the project is complete and the team and PM have disbanded, it's clear that there should still be someone who can manage the day-to-day operations of the application. This is where an *application owner* or *product manager* becomes a critical role that must be identified prior to the project's completion. That person accepts ultimate accountability for the ongoing success of a given application and is the central point of contact for decisions, questions, and future roadmaps. Additional responsibilities of a successful application owner include

■ **Providing technical knowledge:** Although the IT department generally retains responsibility for implementing technical modifications and maintaining the back end of the system, the owner should have sufficient technical understanding to help convey requirements and review system functionality. Additionally, there is always a possibility of conflict between the business, IT, and vendor, and the owner must work closely with staff throughout the organization. Much like the PM, the owner should be able to bridge the gap between business functions and technical implementation to help drive success.

■ **Creating maintenance processes and procedures:** Take a moment to think about some of the apps you commonly use on your phone.

How many of them did you need to take a training course before you could use them? How many of them have user interfaces that vary significantly from one section to another? An application with a consistent look and feel not only makes it easier for end users to adapt to it, but it helps streamline new development, as builders and programmers do not need to reinvent the wheel with every new request. The application owner can play a significant role in drafting maintenance procedures and development standards.

■ **Understanding the long-term goals of the application:** To ensure ongoing success of the application, the owner should have a clear roadmap for where it will fit with the mission of the department or organization in the coming years. This roadmap also defines the types of changes and future project requests that align to that plan. Having a long-term plan will also justify the need for the application to executive stakeholders.

■ **Knowing when it's time to move on:** Even with a well-defined roadmap for development of an application, nothing lasts forever. There will be other players in the marketplace that may offer better solutions at more affordable prices. Or, if the owner has been managing a custom-built solution that begins to feel archaic, it may be time to evaluate other options. Changes to business practices and workflows, new processes and procedures, or even new leadership with a new vision can drive change, and the application owner should always be ready to adapt to that change. Holding onto the past for prosperity sake will serve no benefit.

Obtaining Buy-In from Executive Leadership

Just like the success of anything else, in order to have an effective transition process, you must have a plan that has buy-in from executive leadership. Transitioning projects can be hard, especially if they had prolonged durations with effective project team members and strong project management. Customers will always prefer the path of least resistance, and requiring them to go through a completely different process than was used for the initial implementation may create some initial pushback. Therefore, your executive leadership must understand why this transition is important and fully support the concept of removing the PM and project team members from the ongoing maintenance of the application.

Creating a Transition Plan

Once the groundwork of a formal support process has been established, you can create a formal transition plan for all projects. Although the concept of handoff and transition typically comes towards the end of a project, it's good practice to start early. In fact, you can start the transition planning at the very *beginning* of the project. Let's explore the specific steps you can take during each phase of the project lifecycle to create a framework for a successful handoff.

Project Initiating

While it may seem that there is too little information or planning completed at the very start of a project to even consider how to plan the transition process, there are several tasks that can be started now to help make the eventual handoff even smoother.

1. **Identify resources:** Will the new application require a dedicated support team, or are the existing staffing levels enough? Take the implementation of the Bar Code Medication Administration (BCMA) system, for example. If your requirements included the deployment of new barcode scanners, that's potentially hundreds of new devices that need to be supported. Loose connections, lost equipment, and broken scanners may be quick fixes, but they involve a new workload that must be accounted for early in the project. If there is a need to hire additional field technicians or find space to stock spare parts that may incur an unexpected, long-term cost.

2. **Identify the application owner:** The owner of the system should be involved from the very beginning of the project. If stakeholders are used to this person throughout the process, the eventual handoff from the PM will seem much more expected with a higher level of confidence and comfortability. This also sets the stage for defining the owner's role and responsibility, especially if they will be creating standards and procedure requirements.

3. **Communicate expectations to stakeholders:** No one likes to be surprised by unexpected changes, so communication with your project stakeholders early in the project is important, including the long-term support expectations. Your stakeholders should understand that the PM's job is limited to the initial implementation of the application, and the application owner will assume an ongoing support role once the project is complete.

Project Planning

Starting with the planning phase, the PM will be responsible for all activities within scope to drive the project to completion. While the focus of planning should be the identification of requirements, activities, and project team members, there are a few transition planning activities that should be conducted by the PM:

1. **Confirm activities within scope:** When a project starts, there can be a lot of excitement on the part of stakeholders and end users to implement all the new features and enhancements that are promised by the vendor. However, trying to accomplish everything upfront may not be realistic, or it could require deviating outside of the anticipated cost or schedule for the project. Therefore, the PM must carefully analyze which features are required and which could be deferred until a later phase. Even though the project will close after the scope is complete, there may be an opportunity to have separate phases, projects, or enhancements in the future. This helps the team stay focused on accomplishing specific expectations within a reasonable timeframe. The PM can document items that are specifically out of scope and hand them off to the application owner to consider after the initial implementation project is complete.

2. **Identify all training needs:** Performing training-related tasks may seem like an obvious step before any system implementation, but it's equally important to plan for the training of staff that will provide ongoing support. Do they have the skills needed to maintain this specific application on this particular database? If the vendor will be handling back-end support, what will be the role of the on-site technical team, and what training might they need to perform those duties? The PM should work with the IT team to review the project objectives and perform a gap analysis to determine what training should be built into the project. Since training often requires time and money, it's important to plan for these items early.

3. **Determine roles, responsibilities, and deliverables:** To set the stage for a proper handoff, consider the possible teams that may need to be included in the project. For example, if you need someone to provide ongoing testing support, they should be involved from the beginning to fully understand the requirements, user stories, business workflows, and other background information, so they can adequately prepare testing scripts and understand relationships to other applications in the organization's portfolio. Table 6.2 provides a matrix of additional roles that should be considered during project planning.

Table 6.2   Matrix of Roles and Responsibilities

Role	Responsibility
Product/ application owner	Responsible for the day-to-day processes and procedures of the application, and defines a roadmap for ongoing support and maintenance. Serves as the primary decision maker for the application, provides coordination of changes, and escalates issues to executive leadership.
Executive owner	The highest ranking person to provide ownership of the given application. Responsible for ongoing funding and resource allocation for the application, as well as for making decisions based on questions and issues that have been raised by the application owner. This individual may have limited technical expertise but defends the existence of the application against the mission and vision of the organization.
Application administrator	Responsible for the configuration of the application, including enhancements, features, security, and user access. Ensures the application adheres to CM practices when changes are necessary.
Database administrator	Responsible for the back-end support of the database, including system accessibility, performance, and backup solutions. The database administrator is involved with every upgrade or patch that requires modifications at a database level.
System administrator	Responsible for the back-end hardware and operating system and ensures they meet appropriate security patch levels, antivirus protection, and system availability requirements. Provides support for any backup solutions, including server replication and disaster recovery sites.
Network administrator	Responsible for the infrastructure of the organization that ultimately provides the lowest level support for the application, via wired and/or wireless networks, routers, and switches. The network administrator also has a key role in any integrations with other systems, including the opening and closing of firewall ports and potential network access for remote support.
User support	Responsible for any equipment that is used by end users to access and use the application, including desktops, laptops, barcode scanners, printers, and other peripheral devices.
Help desk	The primary reference point for all questions and issues that may be reported by end users. Responsible for triaging tickets, providing first-call resolution where possible, and escalating issues to appropriate tiers and executive leads, as necessary.

Project Execution

During execution, the defined resources and teams come together to complete the identified tasks to fulfill the needs of the project. Since it's unlikely that a resource will be dedicated fully to the project, PMs often struggle with ensuring that all parties are continually represented at meetings and project gatherings. Operational needs and firefighting will often pull team members to other activities, especially if they do not have any immediate tasks or action items on the project. In these situations, it's incumbent upon the PM to ensure that project activities, decisions, and other outcomes are shared with all parties, either through mandatory stand-up meetings, distribution of meeting minutes, or even a requirement that at least one representative of each team attends every meeting. This is particularly important for those that will be supporting the system, so they can understand the ins and outs of every aspect of the project. It's critical that the PM does not become the only subject matter expert on all things related to the application. When team members are not routinely represented, there is an increased risk of failure by the support team and a high likelihood that end users and stakeholders will continually refer back to the PM after the project is closed for guidance.

One of the key pieces of documentation that should be created at this point is a configuration management (CM) plan. The CM plan provides guidance on how all future changes to the application will be managed. It lists all components of the system that could be changed and the process that must be followed to approve, develop, test, and implement that change. The plan should be reviewed by project sponsors and communicated to all stakeholders. By having a comprehensive CM plan in place, PMs can have additional confidence in removing themselves from the day-to-day workings of the application.

Project Closing

Once all deliverables, objectives, and requirements of the project have been met, the project can begin closeout activities. This is where the actual handoff to the support teams will occur. It's not uncommon for the PM to stay engaged in a project for 2–4 weeks after an application is live to ensure the handoff process is smooth. In fact, by staying engaged, at least on the sidelines, the PM can help uncover any gaps in the transition process that may have developed, so they can be rectified before the project is closed. During closing, project documentation should be archived and distributed, as needed. This may include several references for ongoing support purposes, such as those defined in Table 6.3.

When determining which types of documentation may be necessary for your project, it's important to consider how and when it will be used. All

Table 6.3   Support Documentation

Document	Description	Responsible Party
Knowledge articles	Used by Tier I support to provide quick solutions and answers to potential questions. These articles help increase the likelihood of first-call resolutions or additional guidance on how trouble tickets should be routed.	PM, application owner, application administrator
Service level agreement (SLA)	A document that describes how support will be administered for the application, including response times and system availability requirements. An SLA may include legal ramifications if support agreements are not met.	PM, executive owner, application owner
Memorandum of understanding (MoU)	A document that describes an informal understanding between two parties, such as how remote access rights will be granted to an external party. There are no legally binding requirements in an MoU.	PM, executive owner, application owner
Standard operating procedure (SOP)	A document that provides a set procedure for specific tasks. For example, if there were a request for installing a new workstation for Barcode Administration, there should be a procedure defined on how equipment is configured, how scanners are connected, and how everything is delivered to the customer.	PM, executive owner, application owner
Configuration and change management policies	A policy that ensures all routine changes follow a specific process, including development, testing, and implementation standards. Additional information on change management is included in Chapter 7.	PM, all parties

(Continued)

Table 6.3 (*Continued*)   Support Documentation

Document	Description	Responsible Party
Architecture documentation	A set of documents that describe and diagram how an application is built and integrates with other systems. This could include connections to the server, penetration through firewalls, and interfaces with other applications.	PM, application administrator
User guide	A formal guide, intended for end users, that describes all features of the application and how they should be used.	Vendor, application administrator
Administrator guide	A formal guide, typically authored by the vendor or development team, that provides guidance on how to maintain the system.	Vendor, application administrator
Project summary	A document that provides an overall synopsis on the application or the project and could be used as a central reference point for all other documentation created during the project.	PM

project information should be stored in a centralized location that is accessible to all parties. However, spending hours to create a document that will never be updated or will sit on a shelf gathering dust will do little other than to check a box to satisfy executive leadership. Sometimes the continual use and updating of these documents requires a cultural change in the organization, as well as persistent monitoring by the portfolio office. However, integrating the development and use of these documents into everyday practice will result in stronger IT processes with fewer information silos.

After the handoff process is complete and the project is closed, all resources should be released, including the PM. Once again, communication to stakeholders should reaffirm the commitment to the application owner and other support team members. If customers attempt to circumvent the process by not using the help desk or contacting old project resources directly, it's important to refer them back to the proper methods of submitting their inquiries. It may be necessary to evaluate the performance of the support process on a regular basis to ensure it's still meeting its original objectives. From this point forward, all requests should follow a standard for ongoing maintenance, which is described in more detail in the next chapter.

Chapter 7

Operations and Maintenance

> The ability to roll back the change means that no developer should
> need to leave the office with the application in a "broken" state,
> which would block the progress of the rest of the development team.
>
> **– Andrew Phillips**
> *The IT Manager's Guide to Continuous*
> *Delivery: Delivering Software in Days*

Operations and Maintenance (O&M) is the phase in an application's lifecycle
where it spends the most amount of time and has the most amount of change.
During this period the application must stay available and relevant to the users.
This includes requests for updates as processes and workflows change as well
as the need to upgrade the application and infrastructure when appropriate.

Changes that occur during this phase can be large or small in scope or
work effort. Chapter 3 mentions the analysis of the requests to determine if
they should be managed as a project or through day-to-day operations using
a change control process. Utilizing a workload threshold or total hours to
complete the request can provide guidance on how the change should be
managed. Changes can be identified by a variety of people or groups.

- End users of the application related to wording or functionality changes
- IT department related to improvements or ongoing maintenance of the
  infrastructure
- Regulatory agencies related to updated mandates or reporting
  requirements
- C-suite related to changes to the organization's direction

This chapter will discuss how larger changes are made during O&M projects and how these differ from the initial implementation discussed in Chapter 5. Smaller changes, whether requested or part of maintenance, are managed through configuration management (CM) and release management (RM), which is discussed later in the chapter. At the end, additional activities that occur during O&M will be reviewed, but we will begin with projects.

Projects

The process for requesting new projects was discussed in Chapter 3, which includes requests for all types of projects from new applications to those related to current applications. The main difference is the scope of the project and the tasks for creating documentation are now updating the documents. As mentioned in Chapter 4, the governance committee may not review all project requests depending on their committee charter. During the O&M phase, there will be many activities that will be managed as projects, they may be specific to a single application or they could span multiple applications. They may include

- Upgrading an application to a new version
- Adding additional functionality to an application
- Adding new functionality to an application when available from the vendor
- Refreshing hardware for one or more applications
- Upgrading a database platform across multiple applications

All of these projects are reported to the governance committee in one way or another, either as a request to be evaluated or through the overview of existing projects. Even if the governance committee does not evaluate the project request, a decision should be made on prioritization since resources are always limited. The projects during this phase would follow the same project management methodology described in Chapter 2, but some of the tasks and activities will differ from the initial implementation project described in Chapter 5.

These projects are all occurring on applications that are already in place. Much of the initial analysis and design should have been completed when it was implemented, unless that project occurred prior to instituting those processes. In these cases, there may not have been any evaluation against organizational standards or documentation of the architecture and system design.

The project team is determined by the scope of the project and the tasks to be completed. Some teams should always be included, such as the technical architect, security and privacy team(s), database administrator, system administrator, test team, and post-live support staff. Others may be required based on the status of the system and scope of the project. These may include the interface team, training team, or the network administrator. Each team member will either have defined tasks or may just be requested to be available to resolve any potential issues that may occur.

The technical architect should review the documented system design, if available, and update it as needed for the post-project state. If there is no design documentation, they should be created during the project. As was done during the initial implementation project, the architect should evaluate the application's ability to meet the organizational standards. The standards may change over time, such as having a minimum version of the operating system. If the application was not evaluated when it was first implemented, this is a good opportunity for the analysis to be completed. The resolution of any gaps can be included in the scope of the project or as a risk if they cannot be resolved.

If there is any integration, the interface team should be involved. The integration documentation should be updated, as needed, or created if not present. Even if the scope of the project does not include any changes to the integration, there may be justification to test this functionality anyway. Discussion with the interface team and the sponsor to review what changes are in scope and any potential risks, will identify if testing is needed and should be added to the project plan, if required.

The security and privacy team(s) should also review the documentation and update, if available. If not available, they should create new documentation based on the postproject state of the application. Reviewing the system configuration to ensure it meets organization or mandated standards should also occur. This should include a penetration test and evaluation of any vulnerability once the project changes are complete, but before the go-live or activation date. As with the architecture review, the resolution of any gaps should be included in the scope of the project or added as a risk.

The configuration and build requirements should be documented and approved prior to any changes being made as with all projects. These requirements provide the details for what changes will be made, the tasks to be included in the work breakdown schedule (WBS), and how to determine if the project is successfully completed during project closing. The requirements also feed into the development of the test scripts for the project as well as if any regression testing should occur. As with any project, remember to include time for resolution of any test issues in the schedule.

Any support documentation should be updated based on the changes made during the project. The need for formal training and/or updates to any training materials is based on the specific changes being made. Communication of changes should always occur even if formal training does not. The communication would go to all stakeholders, including end users, the project team, and support staff.

As with any project, planning for the go-live or activation should always begin as early in the project as possible. Since this project is related to application(s) currently in use, the activity will probably require the system to be unavailable to end users while the changes are being implemented into the production environment. Scheduling this activity during a time when the application is not in use would be the best solution, but with some healthcare organizations being a 24 × 7 × 365 business, this may not be possible. In these cases, scheduling the down when usage is at the lowest is the next best option. There should be downtime procedures in place to ensure business continuity. Reviewing these procedures prior to the down will be a good reminder to users on what to do when the application is unavailable and what data should be added when it becomes available again.

The activation checklist, as defined in Chapter 2 and discussed in Chapter 5, is an important piece of planning for the go-live. The checklist not only defines all the tasks that need to be completed surrounding the activation but also helps to calculate the length of time that the system will be unavailable, thereby providing a baseline for downtime planning and communication. The inclusion of go/no-go tasks in the checklist provides the ability to stop and evaluate if the activity should move forward. These are typically added in key locations such as after an upgrade to verify it went as expected before beginning configuration or after testing to verify all critical issues were resolved before activating users. The project schedule should include timing for at least one rehearsal. This is the time for issues to arise and errors to be made since they feed into contingency planning for the production activation activity. The rehearsal should mimic the actual activation as closely as possible. All staff with tasks should be dedicated to this activity, and it is best to utilize a copy of the production system, if possible, to verify timing of the tasks with the same size database. If there were many issues and problems during the first rehearsal, the activation is complex, or it is a high-visibility project, it is recommended to plan for another prior to the actual activation date. Issues encountered during rehearsals may lead to additional tasks. The rehearsals offer a variety of benefits, some of which are listed here.

- The time to find problems, or potential problems, so the team can learn before the production activation.
- Provides duration estimates for individual tasks, the time the system is down, and the entire activation activity.
- Provides experience of completing each task
- Identification of missing tasks
- Identification of any tasks that are out of order
- Identification of risks for individual tasks or the entire activity
- Identification of opportunities to streamline individual tasks or the activity by running some in parallel
- Confirms resource needs

During the rehearsals and activation, the checklist will be updated. Some guidelines to help with the documentation of changes are listed below. The final version of the checklist becomes lessons learned for the next rehearsal or activation within this project or for future projects.

- Nothing from the original checklist will be removed or changed
- Use a different font color to show any modifications to the checklist that occur during the event
- If something is not correct, use strikethrough font to show what is incorrect and change the font color
- If something is missing, add the correct text in the same font color as above
- If a task needs to be moved to a new location in the checklist, use strikethrough colored font for the old location and add a note on why it is not occurring at this time
- New, or moved, tasks should be added using colored font, but do not renumber all subsequent tasks, instead use the number from the task above with "a" or "b" after. This eliminates confusion if members of the team have a hard copy of the checklist by retaining the same numbers for the following tasks.

	Task	Est Duration	Est Start	Actual Start	Actual Finish	Est Finish	Pred	Resource	Comment
70	~~Restore the last backup of the Hog~~	~~20 min~~	~~0836~~			~~0866~~	~~69~~	~~Jennifer~~	~~Moved to a 'better place' in checklist per Jennifer~~
71	*Go / No-go Decision Ready for Upgrade*	10 min	0855	0702	0705	0905	70	Team	
71a	*Verify if there are any ADT orders pending*			0702	0705			Ryan	Queue empty
72	Change Location of DB Server Name in ES Database	5 min	0905	0705	0707	0910	71	Jennifer	
73	Drop Existing Environment	5 min	0910	0710	0715	0915	72	Jim	
74	Create New prod Environment (includes upgrade)	45 min	0920	0715	0748	1005	73	Jennifer	Upgrade
75	Take DB out of dbo use only Mode	5 min	1005	0749	0754	1010	74	Jennifer	
76	Set DB Back to Full	5 min	1010	0754	0758	1015	75	Jennifer	
77	Update System Data	15 min	1015	0759	0817	1030	76	Jennifer	
78	Repoint Services to Upgraded Environment on All Nodes	30 min	1015	0758	0832	1100	76	Jim	
79	Load Updates for Outbound Interfaces	5 min	1100	0832	0835	1105	78	Jim	
80	Start DB Backup (takes approx 60 min to run)	5 min	1105	0835	0840	1110	79	Jim	
81	Test Failover	10 min	1110	0840	0853	1130	80	Jennifer	
82	~~Verify~~ Create HLT Connections	10 min	1130	0853	0900	1140	81	Pat	Need to create new rather than verify
83	DB Backup Complete				0945	1205	80	Jim	60 min after task 80
84	Run DBCC on Prod	45 min	1205	0943	1030	1250	83	Jim	
85	Rebuild DB Server Jobs	40 min	1250	1030	1105	1330	84	Jennifer	
86	*Go / No-go Decision Ready to Configure & Load*	10 min	1330	1105	1107	1340	85	All	
87	Modify Security Groups	10 min	1340	1107	1115	1350	86	Harvey	
88	Assign Key Users to Security Groups	10 min	1350	1115	1127	1400	87	Harvey	
88a	*Turn on Virtual Desktop Access*	*5 min*	*1545*	1130	1135	*1550*	*123*	*Matt*	*Moved up as this can be done earlier than expected*
88b	*Update Settings & Path on All Virtual Desktop Servers*	*60 min*	*1550*	1135	1230	*1650*	*124*	*Matt*	*Moved up as this can be done earlier than expected*
89	Assign Remaining Department Users to Security Groups	20 min	1400	1127	1149	1420	88	Harvey	
90	Verify Report Files	20 min	1400	1128	1145	1420	88	Nicole	
91	*Final Go / No-go Decision*	10 min	1420	1149	1202	1450	89, 90	All	
92	Begin to Upgrade Workstations	---	1450	1205	---	1500	91	Support	Work continues until all workstations are upgraded
93	Start Interfaces	10 min	1450	1202	1212	1500	91	Pat	
94	Start Batch Jobs, in Proper Sequence	5 min	1450	1202	1206	1455	91	Jennifer	
95	Verify Interface Connections & Check Logs	15 min	1500	1212	1230	1515	93	Pat	No issues

Figure 7.1 Partial activation checklist from a rehearsal.

■ It is a recommendation to add "buffer" tasks, especially for lengthy activations. These add small amounts of additional time to the duration as a buffer for tasks that may take longer than expected or when issues take time to resolve. If there are go/no-go tasks, these can be used for this purpose by extending their durations, as with the example shown.

Figure 7.1 shows a partial checklist from a rehearsal for our case study project. In this example, shading is used to highlight where updates where made. Issues would be noted in the Comments column and tracked in a separate issues list. It is noted that the earlier tasks, not shown on this portion of the checklist, were completed quicker than expected as noted by the actual start and end times of the tasks shown.

Project closing should include all the same tasks and activities described in Chapters 2 and 5. The after action report, or completion document, should be reviewed with the sponsors for their approval to close the project. The PM should work with the contracting staff to assist with closing out any contracts specific to this project. The PM does not close out the contracts, but provides input into the defined deliverables or timelines. The application list should be updated based on the changes included in the project scope. Any lessons learned should be documented and once all the project documentation is finalized and archived, the team can be released. Remember to celebrate the successful completion of all projects.

Configuration and Release Management

Change management or CM is the process for evaluating and managing changes to an IT system. RM is the process of planning, controlling, and scheduling the changes through the different stages and environments. These two are often managed together to ensure any change has been evaluated, reviewed, approved, migrated through the different environments, and fully tested prior to being placed into production and verified with the scheduled release. CM and RM are managed with a defined process flow with defined steps and decision points for all changes. For the purposes of this book, we will use CM to refer to both CM and RM.

The CM plan should be defined and approved prior to the end of the initial implementation project of any new application and included in the transition to support communication. Whenever possible, there should be one process flow followed for all changes across all applications. The flow could allow for differences, such as who has the authority to approve requests and the release schedule, but having one basic flow provides consistency and avoids the risk of confusion on what process to follow for the Configuration Change Requests (CCRs). The CM Plan should include who is able to make the request, how the requests are initiated, who receives the request, plus the process for managing the request through the process to completion, or closure if denied.

The options for who can submit a request would be the same as defined in Chapter 3, anyone and everyone; team lead, manager, or supervisor; or designated individuals. Even though these requests are for simple or routine changes, they may still impact all users of the application. Some requests may require review by multiple departments, such as the nursing department requesting a change to the details of a dietary order may need to be reviewed and approved by the nutrition department. It should also be noted that requests could be submitted internally from the IT department, and could be related to the infrastructure, an identified vulnerability or the need to become compliant with changes to organizational or mandated standard requirements. They may also be based on communication from a vendor about a fix to one or more reported issues.

As with project requests discussed in Chapter 3, the CCRs could be submitted through committee, paper form, or electronic means. For these smaller, less complex requests, they may also be communicated in less formal methods, such as a hallway discussion, during a meeting, by email or by phone. It is best to have a defined way to submit the requests to ensure they are actually submitted, and not forgotten, and that all relevant information is included. However, be prepared with a process to handle the less formal requests while reinforcing the correct process.

Having the organization define the threshold of which requests are projects and which are routine changes provides a clear distinction of how to handle each type of request when it is submitted. Since the requestor may not know the work effort to complete their change, it may not always be clear which process to follow, is it above or below the threshold? Communication and collaboration between teams is important as requests come in and are evaluated, they may need to be moved between the two processes once it is determined if it is a project or CCR.

Before you begin to receive requests for changes, it should be determined how each will be managed. This is accomplished by defining the Configurable Items (CIs) for each application. These are any item that can be modified within the system. They can be as detailed as listing each field that can be configured, each piece of a report, or each part of a server. They could also be broader, such as a new clinical document or an update to a current clinical document, without listing each possible item. The level of detail should be enough to identify how each should be managed. The CIs should be documented in a way that allows for searching and modifying as needed. This could be done in a spreadsheet, a simple database, or in a CM-specific application. A baseline should also be documented once the system is live. The baseline is a snapshot of a system's components (such as hardware, operating system, code or configuration, and associated data) to which changes can be applied. The baseline can only be changed through the formal CM process, and a new baseline should be created once a change is made. While this is best practices, most organizations create a new baseline after each release or at some regular interval.

Once the CIs are defined, the levels of configuration control should be defined. This identifies how the changes will be managed through the CM process. Not all changes require the same level or approval, documentation, or processes. Below is an example of four levels of control, the quantity of levels is variable, but each should be defined. Each CI in the list should be identified as being under one of these levels of control. The levels of configuration control should be defined in the CM Plan as well as where the CIs are documented.

Example of CM Control Levels

- Level 1 – item not under version control and does not require documentation or Change Control Board (CCB) approval. An example is adding or removing users from the application.
- Level 2 – item under version control, but do not require a CCR or CCB approval. An example is a test script.
- Level 3 – item under version control, requires a CCR, but does not require CCB approval. An example is updating lab test codes to match lab information system (LIS) for interface.
- Level 4 – item under version control, requires a CCR and CCB approval. An example is updated or new clinical documentation.

It is recommended to have a tool to track the changes through the process. It can be a custom database, a tool with some workflow functionality, or a CM tool that is commercially available. As the request comes in, it is entered into the system creating a CCR. The request should include who requested the change, if any approvals have already been obtained, description of the requested change and impacted applications. It is then assigned to a Subject Matter Expert (SME) for analysis. The analysis should define the requirements for the change, if additional departmental approval is required, the category of the change based on the documented list of CIs and associated level of CM control and what tasks are required to complete the change.

If required, the change would be added to the agenda for the next CCB. This committee reviews CCRs, ensures all information is collected and documented, verifies all impacts are identified, and has the authority to approve or deny the requested change. Oftentimes the committee includes the staff that analyzed or makes the changes along with at least one senior management staff who has the approval authority. There are times when multiple CCBs are required. There may be one specific to the application configuration of the EHR and other primary systems integrated with the EHR, such as the radiology or lab systems. Another CCB could be related to the infrastructure or technical aspects of all systems. If a department supports their own application, they may have a separate CCB to review their change requests. Some CCRs may require review from multiple CCBs depending on the specifics of the request. The CM tool should be able to track which reviews are required so it can be added to the appropriate agenda and the meeting outcomes documented.

As changes are approved, it is assigned to a developer who will make the change. The developer should assign it to a release based on when they anticipate the development will be completed. Each release includes a group of CCRs that will be migrated and tested together. Each release cycle has specific dates for each step. In each cycle, all development is completed by a specific date, and all CCRs included in the release are migrated to the test environment. Each is then tested individually along with basic regression testing. All CCRs that passed testing would then be migrated, or implemented, into the production at the same time followed by a verification that it was migrated correctly as full testing has already been completed. A basic CM process is shown in Figure 7.2.

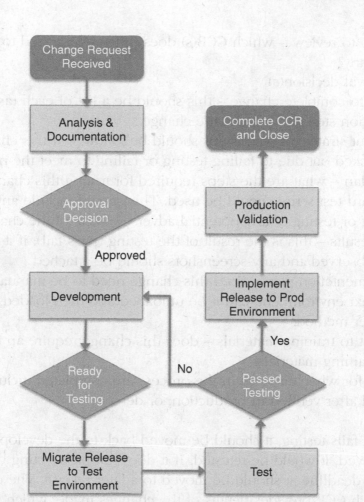

Figure 7.2 Example of a basic configuration and release cycle.

As the CCR is moved through the process, it is important to document each step. The request should also include the following:

- Requestor's name and contact information – this provides a point of contact if additional information is needed or to communicate the approval decision.
- Description of the change requested
- Any approvals received outside of the CCB
- Impacted application(s)
- Responsible parties – this should include names of those working on the CCR, such as the analyst developer, implementer, tester, and approver.

- CCB(s) to review – which CCB(s) does this request need to be reviewed by, if any?
- Approval decision(s)
- Tasks to complete change – this should be a list of each task or configuration step to complete the change.
- Backout strategy – what steps should be followed if this change has to be backed out due to failing testing or failing to meet the need.
- Test plan – what are the steps required for testing this change or what standard test script should be used. This should include any regression testing or testing of any potential adverse effects of the change.
- Test results – this is the result of the testing (pass/fail); if it failed, what was observed and any screenshots should be attached.
- Implementation plan – does this change need to be manually made to the next environment, can it be unloaded and then loaded, or is there another method?
- Impact to training materials – does this change require an update to any training materials?
- Dates for when all steps in the process are completed including when it closed after verified in production, or denied

If any CCR fails testing, it should be moved back to the developer to resolve. Once resolved, it would be retested. If it does not pass testing by the end of the testing deadline, it should be moved to a later release. The documentation on each CCR provides details of the changes made, which assists with the resolution of any identified issues. If necessary, a change or an entire release can be backed out to allow the time to resolve issues and reduce the impact on users. Release notes, a listing of all changes in a release, are shared with users as well as the support staff. The release notes and the details in the individual CCRs support problem management when the support staff is contacted.

In any organization, there will be times when changes will be required to be completed outside of the normal cycle. These could be to fix vulnerabilities, respond to a new regulation, or an immediate need based on a change in patient care such as sudden outbreak requiring a new medication to be added as an orderable item. All CM Plans should have a process for emergency requests. The CCR should still be entered and follow through the process as defined, but at a more expedited rate. The CCB review could be through an ad hoc conference call or via email. Approval is still needed, based on the level of control for the requested change. The change is migrated through the environments and tested outside of the release schedule. The change still needs to be in all environments and fully tested prior to being implemented into the production environment, but the workflow allows it to occur as quickly as possible rather than on the defined release schedule. All emergency requests should be included in the next CCB meeting to communicate the change and as a retrospective review of the request and the applicability of the emergency process.

Another type of request to be considered is how changes made by a vendor will be managed. If the vendor has access to the application, they have the ability to make changes. This would be if they have access to the application in the organization's data center or they are hosting it. The importance of monitoring and controlling changes to avoid adverse effects is applicable no matter who is making the change. These changes should follow the same process flow, from submitting a request to validation in production. If they do not have access to the CM tool, they will need to have a point of contact who does have access. They would work through this resource to submit the request and for notifications as it moves through the steps in the process. Since someone else will be documenting for them in the CCR, the vendor will need to be aware of the process and the details required through each step. It is easier to provide access to the tool, but this is not always possible or desired by the organization.

As mentioned above, the CM process should be as consistent as possible across all applications. This simplifies the request process, management process as well as the roles and responsibilities. If an application, or group of applications, has a different process such as a different CCB or release cycle, then that should be identified and described in the CM Plan. There should be one CM Plan that defines how the change requests will be managed for the entire application portfolio. The CM Plan should include the following information, at a minimum.

- Introduction – defines the purpose of the document, how the organization defines CM, and what applications follow this plan.
- General roles and responsibilities – defines the key roles involved in the CM process, these are described below.
- CCBs – defines what CCBs are available, what their charter is, and what types of requests are reviewed by each.
- Configurable items – defines the categories of CIs, where they are documented, and the process to keep them current, including specific roles and responsibilities.

■ CM and RM – defines the process to be followed from request through to closing, including specific roles and responsibilities.
■ Emergency request process – defines how emergency and/or urgent requests will be handled outside of the above processes.
■ Exceptions – at the end of the document, any exceptions would be managed, such as separate process or release cycle for specific applications or group of applications, management of fixes received from a vendor or how changes made by the vendor are managed.
■ Approvals – includes approval decisions and the dates of those decisions.

The management and control of the CM process requires dedicated staff as well as many who are involved as part of their daily duties. The CM team may report to the Application Portfolio Office or may be a separate office as with a CM Office (CMO). Below is a list of some roles and responsibilities of both direct and indirect resources involved in the CM and RM processes. An organization may choose to break out the SME grouping for the CM Plan to further define their responsibilities.

■ Application Portfolio Office – provides governance and oversight to the CM program.
■ CM Lead – provides leadership and management of the CM program, facilitates all CM activities to ensure the process is followed.
■ Project Managers – implements the CM policies and procedures during the projects, documenting the changes and ensuring the CM team is aware of any changes needed to the CM Plan prior to project closing.
■ Test Team – provides testing for all assigned CCRs and releases, documents the results of the testing, and provides regression testing when requested.
■ SMEs – participate in various levels throughout the CM process and may include requestors, analysts, approvers, developers, and implementers.

It can take time for staff to adopt the CM and RM processes in their daily activities. Constant monitoring and support after they are initially put into place is required to reinforce the new way of making changes. For some, there will be resistance to the level of documentation, waiting for approval or a release, rather than just making the requested or needed change. Support from leadership and ongoing reinforcement will eventually help all staff make this a natural part of their daily work. For some, it just takes longer to get there.

Other O&M Activities

There are many activities that occur, or should occur, during the O&M phase of an application outside of projects and CM–RM. The applications and associated infrastructure will be monitored to ensure availability and to identify any potential issues prior to impacting business continuity. Ongoing support by a help desk is provided for all applications and all users. System backups are monitored and stored both onsite and at an offsite facility. These are just a few of the daily O&M activities that occur during this phase.

For any healthcare organization, the main focus of the IT department's time will be spent on a short list of major applications. The primary focus is typically the EHR, but may also include applications used by the radiology, laboratory, pharmacy, records management, and/or the surgery departments. The application portfolio may contain hundreds of applications beyond the few mentioned above. These remaining applications often have fewer users, are less critical to the organization, or have fewer requests for changes. It is important for all applications within the portfolio to be evaluated on a regular basis to determine usability, reliability, and compliance to current standards.

Best practices note that each application should have an operational review annually, but with the large amount of applications in any portfolio and limited resources, this is rarely done or even possible. The easiest way of completing this review is to include it in all projects. Most of the major applications have some project occurring every year or two related to updates or upgrades. For the others, they would need to be scheduled based on a reasonable cycle relevant to the availability of resources and acceptance of the level of risk.

During the operational review, the application is evaluated for usability, sustainability, and compliance with standards, which are often updated regularly. Meeting with representatives of the user community will identify if it is still being used and still meets their needs. Is there another application in-house that may meet their needs better? The architecture team would evaluate if it meets their standards, which include age of hardware, software versions, and ability to retain support from vendor. The security and privacy team(s) evaluate it from their perspective, which include any vulnerabilities or security risks. As hackers are becoming more advanced, the standards, or requirements, to keep a system secure change. Based on the evaluation, each team should make a recommendation on if the application should be retained, retained with modifications, or disposed. The recommendations are based on if the identified issues or gaps can be resolved, and the steps for resolution lead to the recommended modifications. Senior leadership would review the final document and identified recommendations and provide an approval decision. The approved recommendations may lead to a new request for a project or configuration change. If it is determined that it is no longer in use, or should be disposed, the disposition process should begin, which is described in the next chapter.

Systems monitoring is an ongoing activity to ensure systems are available and to identify potential problems. This is often associated with monitoring the hardware in a data center, but can include interface threads or application's performance. There are often alerts for any change in performance, or interruption, of the network, power, or any issues with the hardware. The staff may also monitor interface traffic to be alerted for any interruption of the dataflow between systems. The goal is for early identification of an issue, so it can be resolved quickly with minimal impact to the business continuity. This activity occurs around the clock everyday. The monitoring staff works closely with the rest of the IT department whenever an issue is identified. For the IT staff, issues with production systems will take precedence over other work, including project assignments.

Providing support to the end users is an important service provided by the IT department. There should be a simple and consistent way to reach the help desk, when a user has a question or needs to report an issue. This puts a huge burden on the support staff to be able to answer questions on any application. They need a simple way to find the right information, to know what questions to ask, to identify the cause of the issue, and to actually provide the support the user requires. The process around transitioning a new application to support is discussed in Chapter 6. It is very important to keep the support documentation current after any change, whether through projects or the CCRs. The support team will often be the first to hear about issues identified by the users. The information about changes from a project or the release notes may provide details to identify the cause of an issue.

There are a variety of activities that may be large enough, in work hours, to be a project, but since they are repeatable, may be managed through the CMO. These could include a regular refresh of an application's environments, rehearsal of system recovery, or the implementation of a package to fix issues provided by the vendor.

It is not unusual for an application that has multiple environments to have them get out of sync due to configuration changes that were made, but abandoned prior to implementing into production. On a regular basis, the environments may be refreshed from a copy of production. This activity requires a backup of production and the removal of all real patient data. The loading of test patient data provides a method of testing and validation without impacting the privacy of real patients. The loading of training data into the refreshed training environment should follow the same process used between classes to keep the data fresh for the new students.

All critical systems should have a business continuity plan as well as a disaster recovery (DR) plan. The business continuity plan defines how the users will continue to do their business when the application is not available. This often relates to going back to paper and printed forms, but should also include what information should be entered into the system when it is back available, who is responsible for entering it, and in what timeframe it is required. The DR plan defines how the system will be restored and any data recovered, if a disaster occurs. This does not relate to a scheduled down when the system is made unavailable for a specific purpose, such as an upgrade. This refers to an unplanned and unexpected system failure. The plan would need to include steps to identify and resolve the cause, but more importantly, the steps to bring the system back up and available to the users while ensuring the database has not been corrupt, and the data is accurate and current. This can be accomplished through redundancy, hot sites, or cold sites. These are described based on availability of separate hardware, application, and data. Once the plan for DR is defined, approved, and put into place, the tasks to recover the system should be rehearsed on a regular basis, at least once or twice a year. This verifies that the process works and that the staff is aware of their tasks and can complete them in the expected timeframe.

Vendors provide fixes to their customers on a regular basis. These are based on reported issues from all customers and are often bundled into a package. This package should be installed into all environments, so they stay current, and would follow the RM process with testing of the included issues and regression testing occurring along the way. They often require the application to be down, or unavailable to the users during the installation. An activation checklist would be used, and typically the majority of the tasks would be consistent each time. Because this is a repeatable process, the CMO team often facilitates it.

There are a significant number of activities that occur during the O&M phase of the application lifecycle, and a few are listed in this chapter. As mentioned earlier, this is the longest phase of the process, with the focus of keeping the system available and relevant to the users while compliant with all regulatory and organizational standards. There are a few processes and plans discussed in this chapter, and it is best practice to review each on a regular basis. The review allows the ability to update them based on experience, what has been working or not working, or based on changing goals and expectations. An application remains in this phase until it is determined that it is no longer used, no longer meets the needs, is unable to be compliant and the risk is unacceptable, or it is unsupportable. When this happens, it should move to the disposition phase.

Chapter 8

Application Disposition

> Have no fear of perfection – you'll never reach it.
>
> **– Salvador Dali**

The decision to discard an application is not an easy one, as there will be many who feel it should be retained forever, even if it is no longer in use. They are often afraid it may be needed at some point in the future or that they will not have access to the data even if is being retained in another format. Moving past these concerns is critical to the final phase in the application's lifecycle and maintaining a reasonable sized and relevant portfolio. Having a clear plan for the disposition process, and communicating the plan, is beneficial to reducing these fears.

There are a variety of reasons to dispose of an application. The most obvious is that it is no longer needed or being used. Other reasons include when the application can no longer meet the mandated or organizational requirements, the risk of being noncompliant is too high, or it is being replaced. The replacement could be with a new application or by adding the functionality to a current one already in place.

As with the rest of the lifecycle events, the disposition should have a defined and repeatable process with specific steps, roles, and templates. An application can have many parts that were put into place when it was initially implemented. If not properly documented, and reviewed, these may be forgotten during the disposition. The first applications identified for disposition are often those that have been in place for a long time and are no longer in use, or the IT department was unaware of and is no longer in place. This occurs while the list of applications in the portfolio is being developed, as discussed in Chapter 1. In these instances, there is probably little, if any, documentation on the configuration. The process should outline all potential parts of an application to ensure each is reviewed, identified if appropriate, and included in the plan to dispose. These could be the obvious parts such as servers, or the less obvious such as open firewall ports or domain accounts.

For most organizations, the repeatable disposition process is defined and put into place at the same time the first application is identified to be disposed. The first key role is the facilitator of the process who will be responsible for managing all the activities and tasks. For some, this may be defined as a project with an assigned PM. If the application is being replaced and data migrated to the new system, the PM for the replacement project might be assigned. For others it might fall into configuration management (CM) with a member of the configuration management office (CMO) in this role. Consistency is key to ensuring that the process is followed for each application and that all parts of the system are removed. The next step is to gather the team, who include members of the following groups who have worked with the application being disposed:

- Architecture
- Security and Privacy
- Network
- System Administrator
- Database Administrator
- Business Analyst
- Web Administrator (if web-based)
- IT Leadership
- Business Application Owner
- Vendor (if vendor hosted)
- Application Portfolio Office

The team will help to identify what will need to be removed, deactivated, or retained for this specific application. If the process is being defined at this time, all potential items should be noted and included in the template being created to ensure they are at least thought of during the evaluation. The contents of a sample template are listed at the end of this chapter.

The process should include the activities and how they fit within the workflow or process flow to ensure they are occurring at the right time and in the right order. One of the first steps is to work with the application owner to identify if any data needs to be retained. If the answer is yes, define the type of data, which will lead to how the data will be retained and stored. Any private or protected data will need to be kept secured while generic reports with de-identified data may be able to be placed on a shared drive.

The facilitator works to document the plan for what to do with the data, retain, migrate, or destroy. If retained, a determination will need to be made on where it will be located and how it will be accessed. If destroyed, it will be important to follow a process that will ensure that data cannot be recovered, such as by degaussing hard drives. If there are backups, the plan should cover how this data will also be destroyed. The simplest option would be through attrition, since they are retained only for a defined period of time. The data will be destroyed when the backup tape, or drive, is reused.

If the vendor hosts any part of the application, they need to be involved in the discussion, planning, and activities to dispose of the application. The main concern for the organization is how their data is managed. If the data is to be destroyed, it is important that it is done in an approved way that ensures it is unrecoverable. If the data is to be returned to the organization, it should be in an agreed-upon format so that it is accessible as expected or able to be easily migrated to the new system. Using a vendor disposition template to document the detailed plan and obtain agreement from the organization and vendor would provide a clear communication on expectations for both parties. The vendor would be asked to document the final disposition of the data. Including the contract staff in the development of the template would be advisable, as this may become a contract document. The vendor disposition document might include the details listed below:

- Contract or award number
- Vendor name
- Application name and version
- Description of data to be returned
- Format of data to be returned and process of secure transmission
- Description of data to be destroyed (include backups)
- Method of destruction
- Expected date of disposition
- Organization's approval signature and date
- Vendor's approval signature and data
- Date data was returned to organization
- Date data was destroyed
- Certificate of media destruction

The disposition plan should define what to do with the application. This should include the application on the server(s) as well as any full client, thin client, or link on the workstations as well as the client on any virtual desktops. The business owner may request to keep the application so they can easily access the data, but this defeats the concept of application disposition and should be discouraged due to required license agreements, support contracts, and maintenance costs.

Finally, the plan should also include what to do with the hardware: retain, reuse, or surplus. Speaking with the system administrators and the architect will identify if the servers will be able to be disposed. They may be used by multiple applications, such as a database server or web server. They may be able to be wiped and reused depending on their age and configuration. The technical staff will also provide input on the additional items and/or exceptions configured for this application. These include the domain accounts and firewall exceptions, as mentioned above, along with items such as interface threads to be removed and other environments that should also be disposed.

Once these are documented, the architecture, security, and privacy teams should review the plan. They should validate that the plans are acceptable and are compliant with the standards and mandates. Once the reviews are complete, the plan should be updated based on the comments or recommendations. The updated and final disposition plan should be discussed with the IT leadership for approval.

With an approved plan for disposition, the tasks are identified, assigned, and tracked to completion. The CM tool used to track the Configuration Change Request (CCR) can be used to track these changes. A CCR would be entered for each task and move through the CM process until complete. They would be identified as approved by the approver of the plan above. The facilitator ensures the work begins on the date identified for disposition and would track the progress of each until all are complete. They will also provide communication to the key stakeholders throughout the process. Once complete, all disposition documentation is archived with the rest of the application's documentation. The application's entry in the portfolio's application list would be updated, and then the application would be made inactive. The application should not be deleted, as this is historical documentation that may need to be referenced in the future. Other tools used to manage applications should also be updated to inactivate or remove the application. These may include the CM tool or monitoring tools.

For the application from our case study, the decision was made to replace the application with functionality now available in a new module from the electronic health record (EHR) vendor. As the project progresses to implement the new module, the work begins to dispose of the BCMA application and migrate the data. The sample template below includes the details for the BCMA application.

Application Disposition Template

Application Name and Version: Barcode Medication Administration v. 5.6
Vendor Name: ABCDEF Corp
Business Point of Contact: Mike S., Pharmacy Director
Date of Disposition Decision: March 13, 2020
Estimated Date of Disposition: September 29, 2020
Date of Final Disposition:
Description of Data:
> The data includes patient demographics, medication order details, dispensing, and administration details.

Plan for Data Disposition:
> Any data not already in the EHR will be migrated during the activation of the new EHR module. Once the migration is complete, there will be 4 weeks for validation prior to disposition in the BCMA system. Degaussing the hard drives of the servers will be the method used to destroy the data. The backup data will be removed through attrition and will take 3 months.

Plan for Application Disposition:
> The application will be removed from the servers when wiped (see below) after the data is migrated and destroyed. The client will be removed from the workstations by the support staff.

Plan for Hardware Disposition:
> The hardware will be wiped per approved method and reused for another application.

Hardware:

Purpose	Server Name	Server IP Address
Application	BCMA_App	10.10.10.10
Database	BCMA_db	10.10.10.11

Tasks and Associated CCRs:

Item	Details	CCR #	Date Completed
Disposition of data	Migrate as above, then dispose	1235	
Disposition of application	Remove client from workstations	1236	
Disposition of hardware	Wipe per approved method	1237	
Active directory or system accounts	Admin account to be removed from active directory	1238	
Active ports	Close port XXX	1239	
Firewall exceptions	None		
Web addresses	None		

Plan Reviews:

Review	Comments and Recommendations	Date of Review
Architecture		
Security and privacy		
Leadership		

Approval Decision:

☐ Approved   ☐ Denied

_____   _____   _____

Name   Title   Date

General Comments:

Any general comments would go here. This would include notes as the work progresses, any issues encountered as well as their resolutions.

Appendix A: Earned Value Measurement

Term	Formula	Definition
Planned Value (PV)		The portion of the total estimated costs to be spent on an activity during a given period.
Actual Cost (AC)		The total amount spent on a task up to the current date or total direct and indirect costs from work on an activity during a given period.
Earned Value (EV)	EV = PV to date x RP	The budgeted cost of work completed as of the current date is based on the planned cost and the rate the team is completing the work to date.
Rate of Performance (RP)	RP = Actual Work/ Planned Work	The ratio of actual work completed to the percent of work planned to be completed at any given time.
Cost Variance (CV)	CV = EV – AC	The difference between the work that has been accomplished (in dollars) and how much was spent to accomplish it.
Schedule Variance (SV)	SV = EV – PV	The difference between what was planned to be completed and what has actually been completed as of a specific date.

(Continued)

Term	Formula	Definition
Cost Performance Index (CPI)	CPI = EV/AC	The ratio of earned value to actual cost. This ratio is used to estimate the projected cost of completing the project. If the CPI equals 1, the actual costs are equal to the budget. If the CPI is <1, the actual costs are over budget. If the CPI is >1, the actual costs are under budget.
Schedule Performance Index (SPI)	SPI = EV/PV	The ratio of earned value to planned value. This ratio is used to estimate the projected time to completion of the project. The outcome is similar to the CPI. If the SPI equals 1, the project is on schedule. If the SPI is <1, the project is behind schedule. If the SPI is >1, the project is ahead of schedule.
Percent Complete (%Comp.)		The progress to completion of a task and is related as either EV/BAC, or simply the physical progress towards completion. If formal earned value measurements are not required, this value is often estimated by the task resource.
Budget at Completion (BAC)		The total budget allocated for the project.
To-Complete Performance Index (TCPI)	TCPI = (BAC − EV)/ (BAC − AC)	Indicates the CPI required throughout the remainder of the project to stay within the stated budget.
Estimate at Completion (EAC)	EAC = BAC/CPI EAC = EAC − AC EAC = AC + ((BAC − EV)/ CPI)	A forecast of total costs that will be accrued by project completion based on past cost performance trends.

Appendix B: Acronyms and Abbreviations

ADT	Admission, Discharge, and Transfer
APO	Application Portfolio Office
BCMA	Bar Code Medication Administration
CCB	Change Control Board
CCR	Configuration Change Request
CM	Configuration Management
CMO	Configuration Management Office
COTS	Commercial Off the Shelf
CR	Change Request
DBA	Database Administrator
DR	Disaster Recovery
EHR	Electronic Health Record
EVM	Earned Value Management
GA	General Availability
IT	Information Technology
IVV	Independent Validation and Verification
LIS	Laboratory Information System
MOU	Memorandum of Understanding
O&M	Operations and Maintenance
PHI	Protected Health Information
PII	Personal Identifiable Information
PM	Project Manager
PMI	Project Management Institute
PMO	Project Management Office
PPO	Project Portfolio Office
RM	Release Management

SaaS	Software as a Service
SDLC	Software Development Lifecycle
SLA	Service Level Agreement
SME	Subject Matter Expert
UAT	User Acceptance Testing
WBS	Work Breakdown Structure

References and Additional Reading

Books

Aiello, Bob and Leslie A. Sachs. *Configuration Management Best Practices: Practical Methods that Work in the Real World*. Upper Saddle River, NJ: Addison-Wesley, 2011.

Baschab, John, John Piot, and Nicholas G. Carr. *The Executive's Guide to Information Technology*, 2nd ed. Hoboken, NJ: John Wiley & Sons, 2007.

Cole, Rob and Edward Scotcher. *Brilliant Agile Project Management: A Practical to Using Agile, Scrum and Kanban*. Harlow, England: Pearson, 2015.

Garets, Claire McCarthy, Douglas Eastman, and David E. Garets. *Change Management Strategies for an Effective EMR Implementation*. Chicago, IL: Healthcare Information and Management Systems Society, 2010.

Houston, Susan M. *The Project Managers Guide to Health Information Technology Implementation*, 2nd ed. Boca Raton, FL: CRC Press, Taylor & Francis Group, 2018.

Kumar, Sumeet. *Leading Courageously with Lean Management: The Missing Link to Organizational Culture*. New York: Productivity Press, 2017.

Manas, Jerry. *The Resource Management and Capacity Planning Handbook: A Guide to Maximizing the Value of Your Limited People Resources*. New York: McGraw-Hill, 2015.

Note, Margot. *Project Management for Information Professionals*. Waltham, MA: Chandos Publishing, 2015.

Project Management Institute *A Guide to the Project Management Body of Knowledge (PMBOK Guide)*, 6th ed. Newtown Square, PA: Project Management Institute, 2017.

Schwalbe, Kathy. *Information Technology Project Management*. Australia: Thomson/Course Technology, 2014.

Wager, Karen A., John Glaser, Frances Wickham Lee, and Karen A. Wager. *Health Care Information Systems: A Practical Approach for Health Care Management*. San Francisco, CA: Jossey-Bass, 2009.

Websites

Health IT Dashboard. Office-Based Physician Electronic Health Record Adoption. Dashboard.healthit.gov. 2017. Accessed June 11, 2019. https://dashboard.healthit.gov/quickstats/pages/physician-ehr-adoption-trends.php.

Landi, Heather. Survey: Nearly·All U.S. Hospitals Use EHRs, CPOE Systems. Healthcare Innovation. September 11, 2017. Accessed June 11, 2019. www.hcinnovationgroup.com/clinical-it/news/13029134/survey-nearly-all-us-hospitals-use-ehrs-cpoe-systems.

Presentation

Houston, Susan and Ryan Kennedy. Project management: Prioritizing, managing and controlling your project and application portfolios. *Healthcare Information and Management Systems Society (HIMSS) Global Conference*, Orlando, FL. February 11, 2019.

Index

Printed in the United States
by Baker & Taylor Publisher Services